People Who Changed American History

# 100 African Americans Who Changed American History

Chrisanne Beckner

WORLD ALMANAC® LIBRARY

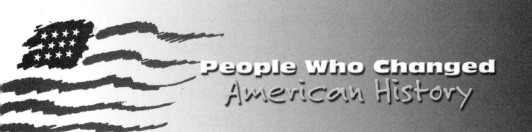

**Please visit our web site at: www.worldalmanaclibrary.com**
**For a free color catalog describing World Almanac® Library's list of high-quality books and multimedia programs, call 1-800-848-2928 (USA) or 1-800-387-3178 (Canada). World Almanac® Library's fax: (414) 332-3567.**

**Library of Congress Cataloging-in-Publication Data**

Beckner, Chrisanne.
[100 African-Americans who shaped American history]
100 African Americans who changed American history / by Chrisanne Beckner.
p. cm. — (People who changed American history)
Includes index.
ISBN 0-8368-5767-4 (lib. bdg.)
1. African Americans—Biography—Juvenile literature. 2. African Americans—History—Juvenile literature. I. Title. II. Series.
E185.96.B365 2005
920'.009296073—dc22
[B] 2004057736

This North American edition first published in 2005 by
**World Almanac® Library**
330 West Olive Street, Suite 100
Milwaukee, WI 53212 USA



Editor: Ruth DeJauregui
Designer: Ruth DeJauregui
World Almanac® Library editor: Betsy Rasmussen
World Almanac® Library art direction and cover design: Tammy West

Cover image: Harriet Tubman

Photo credits: © Tony Chikes: all illustrations; © MPI/Getty Images: cover, 21, 22; © Library of Congress/Time & Life Pictures/Getty Images: 31; © Frank Driggs Collection/Getty Images: 61; © John Kobal Foundation/Getty Images: 65; © Hulton Archive/Getty Images: 67, 80; © Stan Wayman/Time & Life Pictures/Getty Images: 74; © William Philpott/Getty Images: 79; © Gjon Mili/Time & Life Pictures/Getty Images: 82; © Don Hogan Charles/New York Times Co./Getty Images: 93; © Paul J. Richards/AFP/Getty Images: 96; © Central Press/Getty Images: 98; © James Keyser/Time & Life Pictures/Getty Images: 100; © Jacques Collet/AFP/Getty Images: 102; © Trevor Humphries/Getty Images: 107



Printed in the United States of America

1 2 3 4 5 6 7 8 9 09 08 07 06 05

About the Author: Chrisanne Beckner is a writer living in Sab Francisco, California. She has also written *100 Great Cities of World History* and edited several other books.

# TABLE OF CONTENTS



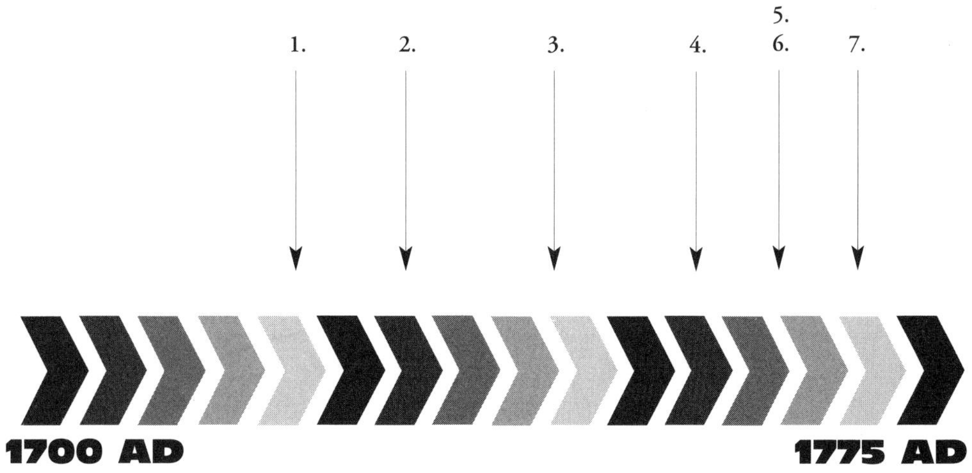

# TABLE OF CONTENTS



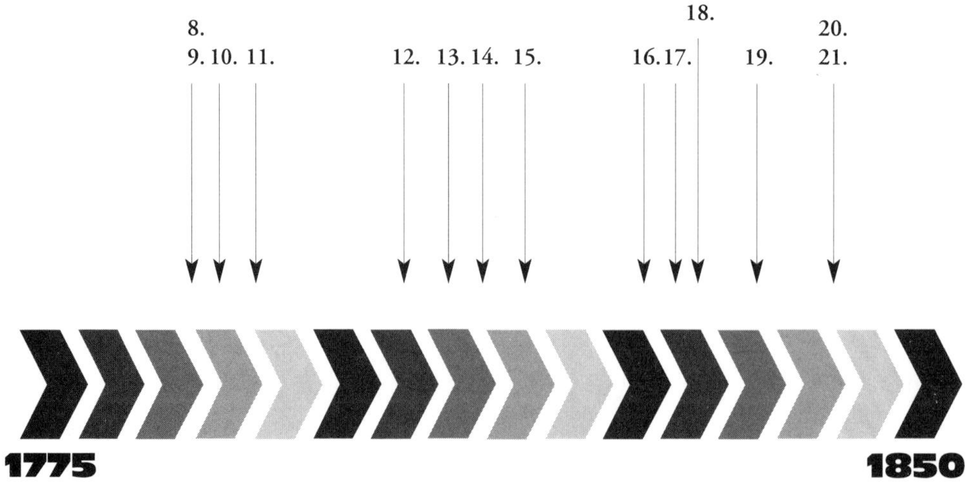

# TABLE OF CONTENTS



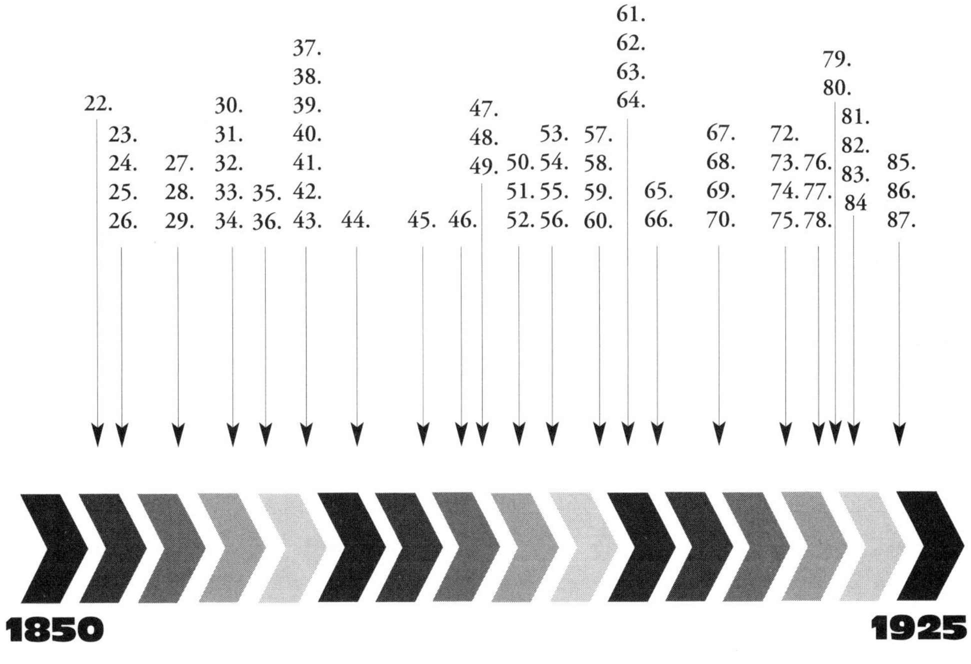

# TABLE OF CONTENTS



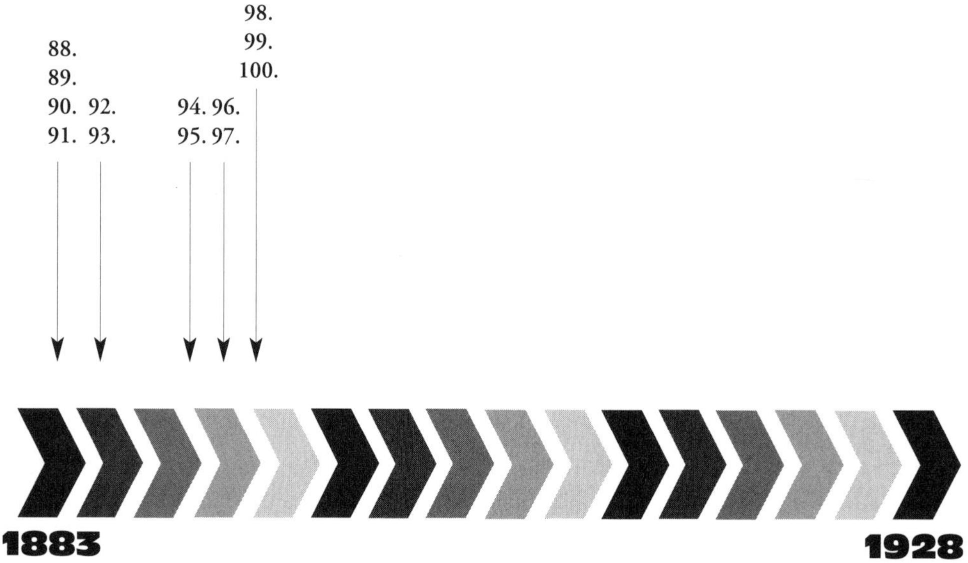

# ALPHABETICAL TABLE OF CONTENTS

# 1. CHRISPUS ATTUCKS
(1723–1770)

Crispus Attucks, one of the first patriots to give his life in the struggle for American independence, was born in Massachusetts in 1723. With African and Natick Indian ancestors, Attucks's only chance for freedom was to escape from slave owner William Brown. At the age of twenty-seven, Attucks ran away from Brown's home and joined the crew of a boat sailing away from Boston Harbor. For the next twenty years, Attucks was a man of the sea.

As a sailor on cargo ships and whalers, Attucks developed an independence that not only made him a brave leader among sailors but a leader of patriot revolutionaries as well. On the night of March 5, 1770, at the age of forty-seven, Attucks's dedication to librerty made American history.

Tension between the Boston patriots and British soldiers was boiling that spring. British forces were installed to impose order—a fragile order at best—and the ubiquitous threat of violence kept colonists in a high state of agitation. Hugh Montgomery, one of the British soldiers, was guarding the Customs House when a young boy came up and insulted him. Montgomery struck out and injured the boy, whose cries rang through the streets, calling people from their homes. Crispus Attucks came forward. He decided immediately, living in a society already on the verge of revolt, that this act of violence would not be tolerated.

**Chrispus Attucks**

Within minutes, a crowd had gathered behind Attucks, who was heading straight for the Customs House. He approached Hugh Montgomery personally, insults were exchanged, and soon the crowd took up chunks of ice and snowballs that they threw at the British soldier.

Twelve others appeared, armed and ready, but Attucks, wielding a heavy stick, yelled, "Don't be afraid. Knock 'em over. They dare not fire." It was the first cry of the coming revolution.

The soldiers responded in panic, firing wildly into the crowd, killing Attucks and his supporter Samuel Gray immediately. Nine other men were shot in the ensuing battle. Three of them died.

The crowd was soon subdued, but news of the massacre was electric, igniting outrage and shock along with a new sense of purpose. Thousands came to Attucks's funeral, and seven British soldiers were brought to trial for murder, though each was exonerated.

This first revolt would come to be known as the Boston Massacre, one of the first battles to mark the beginning of the American Revolution. John Adams later said, "On that night, the foundations of American independance were laid."

It was Crispus Attucks who cared enough about personal freedom to risk his life for its reward, even if that reward would only be available to those who came after.

# 2. BENJAMIN BANNEKER
(1731–1806)

Benjamin Banneker was one of America's first and finest scientists, as well as one of Thomas Jefferson's great influences. He was born in 1731 to the daughter of Molly Walsh, a former indentured servant in her native England. Both mother and daughter purchased slaves in Maryland who later became their husbands.

Benjamin loved learning to read and write from Molly's family Bible, but once he began attending a Quaker school, he knew his great love was mathematics. He studied so passionately that he would create his own problems just for the joy of solving them.

His early interest made him a wise inventor, when he decided to re-create a pocket watch he saw on a traveling salesman. Since no watches existed in America, Benjamin Banneker used all his mathematical skill to develop plans, make the right calculations, and personally carve each gear of the first American watch. Made entirely of wood, Banneker's watch ran perfectly for more than forty years.

**Benjamin Banneker**

Banneker's passion for exactness also extended to the study of astronomy. In 1789, he predicted a solar eclipse that, to the surprise of skeptical astronomers, occurred just as he'd said it would on April 14.

His brilliance extended also into the realm of human rights. After reading Thomas Jefferson's doctrine that "all men are created equal; that they are endowed by their Creator with certain unalienable rights, and that among these are life, liberty, and the pursuit of happiness," and knowing that Jefferson owned slaves, Banneker was moved to write back. In an extremely eloquent letter, Banneker told Jefferson that African Americans were equal to white Americans in intelligence, and therefore equally entitled to rights and privileges. As proof, he included a copy of his almanac, a yearly publication documenting holidays, coming eclipses, and the hours of sunrise and sunset. Banneker's almanac included essays on the abolition of slavery as well.

Jefferson wrote back with a new egalitarian stand on the issue of race. A respectful friendship formed between the two men and remained strong even after Jefferson became the president of the United States.

Banneker went on to become one of the foremost astronomers of his age, as well as one of the men chosen to lay out the new capital city of Washington, D.C., in 1791. After Pierre Charles L'Enfant, the French city planner, quit and took all his plans for the new capital city back to France, it was Banneker who reproduced them from memory.

In October, 1806, after a lifetime of scientific discovery, Benjamin Banneker died, leaving Americans a more accurate vision of "freedom for all."

# 3. ELIZABETH FREEMAN
(1742–1829)

**Elizabeth Freeman**

Elizabeth Freeman, one of the most successful abolitionists of the eighteenth century, was raised in Massachusetts during very exciting times. As a young slave in the house of Colonel John Ashley, Freeman heard the frequent family discussions of a possible freedom from British rule. As the tension between the colonists and the British continued to grow, and Thomas Jefferson's Declaration of Independence became the topic of everyone's conversation, Elizabeth Freeman became convinced that she too was free.

In 1781, Freeman, deciding to prove her theory, ran away from the Ashley home and contacted a young lawyer named Theodore Sedgwick. She explained that since the signing of the Declaration of Independence and the passage of the Massachusetts Constitution, she too was a free woman. Though she knew it was dangerous, she refused to return. Sedgwick was won over by Freeman's argument and agreed to represent her in court.

That same year, the county court in Great Barrington, Massachusetts, heard such eloquent statements from both Freeman and Sedgwick that not only was Elizabeth Freeman granted her freedom, but based on the state constitution, slavery was declared illegal. Elizabeth Freeman was given thirty shillings in damages from the Ashley family, as ordered by the judge, and she went to work for the Sedgwick family. Earning her own living as a free woman, she stayed on until her death in 1829.

Because of Freeman's courage and commitment, slavery was outlawed in the state of Massachusetts and later in the rest of the nation. It was women and men like Elizabeth Freeman and Theodore Sedgwick who finally validated the Declaration of Independence in the United States. Without them to begin the fight for equality, the essential truth of the document might have been lost.

# 4. PHILLIS WHEATLEY
(1753–1784)

Phillis Wheatley, a celebrated poet until her untimely death, was born in Africa and stolen by slave traders at the age of seven or eight. Deposited in rags from a slave ship in Boston, she was purchased by John Wheatley as a companion for his wife Susannah.

From the beginning, Phillis was a great lover of words. Susannah taught her to read and write, and within a year and a half, Phillis Wheatley was a fluent master of the English language. At fourteen, after devouring all the books she could find, (preferring Alexander Pope above all others), Phillis Wheatley wrote her first poem, which historian Lerone Bennett called "a blank verse eulogy of Harvard University." Printed in Boston in 1770, it was to begin her life as an internationally celebrated writer.

In 1772, due to her frail health, the Wheatleys freed Phillis and sent her to England, where she was hailed as a prodigy. Her book, *Poems on Various Subjects, Religious and Moral*, was published, with a forward signed by men such as John Hancock, and Phillis was invited to meet the queen. But word reached her that Susannah was ill, and Phillis returned to Boston at once. Susannah Wheatley died in 1774, and Phillis remained at the Wheatley house to care for John, never ceasing to write.

In 1775, she wrote a poem in honor of the new commander in chief of the American Army, General George Washington. When Washington re-ceived the poem, he sent a letter of thanks that praised the work as "elegant" and "striking," while also stating that it was only for fear of appearing vain that he did not publish it himself. Phillis was then invited to Cambridge, where she was entertained by the Washington family.

Though Phillis Wheatley moved freely as a poet (as did Lucy Terry Prince, the first African American to publish poetry), she had to face the severity of racism.

After the death of John Wheatley, Phillis Wheatley married a gentleman named John Peters, who turned out to be a poor match for her. The last few years of Phillis Wheatley's life were spent in ill health and desperate poverty. The couple lost their first and second child, and Phillis was working in a boarding house as a charwoman when she and her third child died within hours of one another.

Though Phillis Wheatley's death was tragic, her poems were great celebrations of freedom, Christianity, and the lives of great men. They have became part of the respected body of literature that survives to illuminate the lives and spirits of early Americans.

**Phillis Wheatley**

# 5. PAUL CUFFE
(1759–1817)

Paul Cuffe was the founder of the African nation of Liberia, the first free nation in Africa employing the principles of Western countries. He was born free on Cuttyhunk Island in Massachusetts. His father was a former slave who married a Wampanoag Native American woman, and together they raised a boy who, by the age of sixteen, had left home to earn his living by the sea. Cuffe was well-suited to this life and became wealthy from the success of his fishing, whaling, and shipping expeditions. His fleet of ten ships sailed to both the European and African continents regularly.

Though he was a wealthy and powerful businessman in America, Cuffe believed that only in Africa could he live truly free from racism, which had not ceased even after the American Revolution. In 1778, with the signing of the Massachusetts Constitution, Cuffe and all other African Americans, as well as all Native Americans in Massachusetts, lost their right to vote. It was an indignity that abolitionists could not accept quietly.

In response, Cuffe stopped paying taxes. He argued that African Americans and Native Americans were on the front lines of the Revolutionary War with all other Americans. They were buying their country with their lives. In 1783, a Massachusetts court voted in agreement with Cuffe and his supporters and reinstated voting rights to all free, tax-paying African Americans.

This victory was the first political one for Paul Cuffe, who went on to build a school on his farm for the children of his community before launching the plan that earned him the name "Father of the Black Back-to-Africa Movement."

In 1810, Cuffe made his first trip to Sierra Leone in Africa with the purpose of founding an African American colony that would support itself through trade with the United States. Five years later, he traveled back with thirty-eight of the first settlers of a new country. Once the American Colonization Society convinced Congress to acquire African lands for the settlement of free African Americans, the country of Liberia, named for "liberty," was founded. (The American Colonization Society, founded by white slave owners, was an organization dedicated to moving free African Americans to African colonies in order to deflect their attention from the abolitionist movement in America.)

Though more than 14,000 Americans returned to Africa over the next thirty years, many of Cuffe's contemporaries, including Richard Allen (see no. 6) and Absalom Jones, stayed to protect the roots of the African American community fighting for freedom in America.

**Paul Cuffe**

# 6. RICHARD ALLEN (1760–1831)

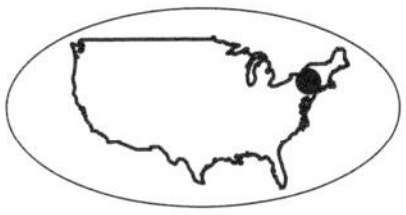

**Richard Allen**

Richard Allen, who would found one of the first African American Christian churches, was born in Philadelphia, but he was sold to the Stockley family of Delaware along with the rest of his family. A bright child, Allen taught himself to read and write. He worshiped at Methodist church meetings, and at the age of twenty-three, with the money he earned as a day laborer, purchased his freedom and began traveling with a minister who taught him to preach.

By the age of twenty-six, he returned to Pennsylvania, and he began holding prayer meetings. Like other Methodists, Allen and his friend Absalom Jones worshiped at St. George's Methodist Episcopal Church in the city. Within a year of Allen's arrival in Philadelphia, St. George's had become so popular that the church ruled that black congregationalists must retreat to the back of the gallery. Absalom Jones was asked to move during prayer and forcibly pulled from his knees when he asked if the prayers could be concluded first. Rather than endure such treatment, Jones, Allen, and the rest of the African American congregation left St. George's and formed the Free African Society. This event inspired Allen to found his own church where African Americans could worship freely.

Through laboring as a shoemaker, Allen bought a plot of land and began construction. By 1794, the Bethel African Methodist Episcopal Church (AME) was complete. Allen was named its first bishop.

Attracting a huge congregation, the AME grew past its borders, severing its ties with the Methodist Church and uniting with other African Methodist churches. Soon, the expanded congregation included thousands of members united under one national organization. The church thus became the foundation of the African American community, providing a training ground for black leadership and unifying efforts opposing slavery and racialdiscrimination.

Churches have remained an invaluable institution in African American communities because of the work of men like Allen and Jones, who counted freedom of religion among the highest rights of men.

# 7. JAMES FORTEN
(1766–1842)

**James Forten**

James Forten, who was a wealthy businessman and abolitionist instrumental in opposing the forcible deportation of African Americans, grew up the son of free parents in Philadelphia. He left his family at the age of fifteen to become a powder boy during the American Revolution. When his ship was captured by the British, not only did Forten refuse to denounce his country in return for his freedom, he gave his one chance to escape to a younger boy and stayed in captivity until a prisoner exchange was arranged.

This same tenacity made Forten a valuable employee to Robert Bridges, a sailmaker in Philadelphia who named Forten a foreman supervising forty men within two years of employment. When Bridges passed away, Forten purchased the business, made it one of the city's most profitable, and invented a new sail-making device that earned him great respect, as well as wealth.

As a popular community businessman, Forten was one of the strongest voices against the forced colonization of African Americans. When the American Colonization Society, made up primarily of white slave owners, attempted to pass legislation deporting all free African Americans to Africa, Forten spoke out. He gave a speech at the Bethel Church in Philadelphia, stating that it was their ancestors who had enriched the land with their blood and sweat. Forten believed that African Americans had to stay and continue to fight for freedom within their new country. With this statement, he gained an enormous following within his community.

Forten's support for African Americans did not stop there. He supported Absolom Jones and Richard Allen (see no. 6) by vacating the St. George Church in protest, and he protested Pennsylvania's attempt to restrict African American immigration from the South. He pledged both his wealth and his name to his ideals and went on to found the Pennsylvania Augustine Society "for the education of people of colour." He also authored an influential text entitled "A Series of Letters by a Man of Color."

Forever fighting for the improved position of African Americans, Forten didn't live to see the end of slavery, though his words prove that he never doubted its coming: "The spirit of freedom is marching with rapid strides and causing tyrants to tremble . . . May America awake."

# 8. SAMUEL E. CORNISH (1795–1858) JOHN RUSSWURM (1799–1851)

John Russwurm and his partner Samuel Cornish founded the first black newspaper in the United States in 1827. *The Freedom Journal*, the first record to emerge and develop as a written chronicle of black America, was the prototype for other influential papers. *Colored America* was first printed in 1837 and *The North Star* was published by Frederick Douglass (see no. 14) in 1847.

Linking people in various African American communities, *The Freedom Journal* was the first paper to bring to light the details of lynchings, to disseminate abolitionist news, and to link the United States to Africa by reporting on social conditions on that continent as well.

To clarify the intent of their publication, Russwurm and Cornish proclaimed their goals in their first editorial: "The publication of this journal; the expediency of its appearance at this time, when so many schemes are in action concerning our people—encourage us to come boldly before an enlightened publick (sic). For we believe that a paper devoted to the dissemination of useful knowledge among our brethren, and to their moral and religious improvement, must meet with the cordial approbation of every friend of humanity. . . . We wish to plead our own cause. Too long have others spoken for us. Too long has the publick (sic) been deceived by misrepresentations in things which concern us dearly. . . ."

Cornish and Russwurm lived by the same ideals that inspired their readers. Working tirelessly for the rights of all Americans, they used their journal and their lives to hasten the abolition of slavery and educate great men and women. Linked throughout the world on issues of rights and freedoms within African and African American populations, their readers grew into a unified front that would eventually lead to freedom for all.

**Samuel E. Cornish & John Russwurm**

# 9. DRED SCOTT
(1759–1858)

**Dred Scott**

Dred Scott, a slave who sued for his freedom and saw his case all the way to the U.S. Supreme Court, began life under the ownership of Peter Blow of Southampton County, Virginia. After Blow's death, Dred Scott was sold to a U.S. Army surgeon named John Emerson. Emerson and his wife traveled to Fort Armstrong in Illinois and took Scott with them, though Illinois had already abolished slavery. From there, the Emersons and Scott traveled to Wisconsin, another free state, and again Scott was illegally kept, under Emerson's assertion that he was a resident of Missouri who was only temporarily traveling under the command of the U.S. Army.

Without resistance, the Emersons took Scott back to Missouri in 1839. Mr. Emerson died in 1843, and Dred Scott attempted to buy his freedom from Mrs. Emerson. When she refused to free him and his family, Scott sued, claiming that for years he'd been enslaved in free states and should now be granted the freedom he'd been due years earlier.

Though he lost the first case, Scott persevered, taking his case to a second court in St. Louis. This time he won, only to have the ruling overturned by the Missouri Supreme Court in 1852, two years after the St. Louis court had handed him the right to freedom. To support the next and final case, Dred Scott accepted the help of friends, family, and white abolitionists who prepared him for the U.S. Supreme Court.

This ruling was the most bitter. The U.S. Supreme Court denied Scott the rights of an American citizen and, therefore, the right to sue. On March 6, 1857, Judge Roger B. Taney ruled that slaveowners and their property could travel freely through any state. All antislavery laws were declared unconstitutional, and Dred Scott died two years later in Missouri.

To many, Scott's case was the last straw. Those who'd believed that slavery could be abolished without violence were convinced otherwise. The backlash was extreme, and Scott's case strengthened the commitment to freedom that finally pushed the United States into civil war, the war held responsible for the abolition of slavery nationwide.

# 10. SOJOURNER TRUTH
(1797–1883)

Born in Hurley, New York, as Isabella Baumfree, Sojourner Truth was sold four times before she ran away permanently in 1826. Always passionate, Isabella went to New York City, where she worked and followed her strong religious impulses into various groups and cults, including one publicly disgraced for its questionable moral practices.

But in 1843, Isabella Baumfree went through a transition that left her forever the committed advocate of justice for all men and women. A voice from God told her, in her own words, "to travel up and down the land showing the people their sins and being a sign unto them." God told her to take the name Sojourner, and when she asked for a second name, she was told to take Truth, for she would be bringing the truth about slavery, religion, and women's suffrage to the American public for the rest of her life.

A gutsy, bold, and dynamic speaker, Truth traveled throughout the country, gaining the attention of some of the brightest minds dedicated to the abolition of slavery. Though illiterate, Truth had a fanaticism and a presence that was unshakable. She was bold enough to chastise Frederick Douglass (see no. 14), inspire awe in Harriet Beecher Stowe, and shame slaveowners who tried to oppose her. She had "power and a quick, incisive mind that reduced things to their essentials," as Lerone Bennett said, and, as Stowe said, "an unconscious superiority."

Though her focus was always on teaching the truth, her courage led her to action as well. The money she made by lecturing and singing went to African American soldiers at the beginning of the Civil War, and when newly freed slaves suffered through the transition, she went to Arlington, Virginia, to help them move easily into their own lives.

She was also the original freedom rider. In 1865, when Congress voted to end segregation, Truth was the first to force the subject with horse car drivers. When they refused to stop for her, she went into the middle of the street, waving her arms and demanding, "I want to ride! I want to ride!" When a crowd gathered to support her, the next car was forced to stop. Truth climbed aboard and sat like stone, refusing to budge when the conductor tried to throw her off. Failing to remove her, he gave in, but Truth made sure he was later arrested and fired from his job. Once again, she had forced the point of desegregation into the lives of Americans.

She continued roaming and teaching until the end of her life. At that time, she was still trying to purchase enough land in the new western territories to support freed slaves ready to build new lives.

**Sojourner Truth**

# 11. NAT TURNER
(1800–1831)

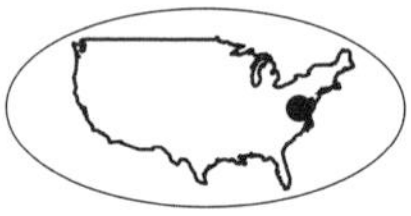

**Nat Turner**

Nat Turner, the man who led the 1831 slave uprising, was born to an African born slave of such self-determination that she felt she could not bear to bring another slave into the world. It was said that she had to be held away from hurting him.

Along with her hate for slavery, Turner's mother also passed on a respect for religion and ritual. From childhood, Nathaniel Turner was a deeply religious person who felt he was chosen by God for a special purpose. Dedicated to prayer and the visions and voices that stirred him, Nat grew into a powerful community leader and a commanding learned man. In the service of a religious life, Turner denied himself all vice and stayed apart from society. Eventually, a mixture of awe and curiosity led people to call him "the Prophet."

In 1831, the Prophet received a vision. He is said to have heard a voice that told him to "arise and prepare myself and slay my enemies with their own weapons." After years of faithfully preaching to his community, Nat Turner gathered four men around him and began to plan the rebellion that stands as one of the most meaningful events on the road to the abolition of slavery.

At the appearance of the promised sign, the solar eclipse of February, 1831, Nat Turner and his men gathered to plot their rebellion. Through interruptions and postponements, it was stifled until the appearance of the second sign, a bluish haze over the Sun in August of 1831. At that time, they decided they could wait no longer. By God's sign they entered the house of Turner's master and murdered him and his family. This was the first act of a rebellion that would kill fifty-seven whites in twenty-four hours and attract seventy rebels who terrified the white population for months after.

On their way to Jerusalem, Virginia, Turner met his first opposition. Nat's men were defeated and scattered, and Nat went into hiding for two months, eluding capture and intensifying a terror that rolled into hysteria over the eastern and southern states.

While Nat Turner hid, whites gathered in heavily armed groups and attacked armed, unarmed, and innocent African American families. Nat Turner was finally caught and brought to trial, where he pleaded "not guilty" and was sentenced to death. He predicted the Sun would not shine on the day of his execution, and a surprising thunderstorm rose up and swept across the Sun as Turner hung from a rope in Jerusalem, Virginia.

Though the bloodshed was massive, Nat Turner managed to give a reality to the passion of black Americans who were fighting to abolish slavery in America. Nat Turner was an example of resistance and a sign to white America that freedom was imperative and would come for them one way or another.

# 12. MARTIN R. DELANY (1812–1885)

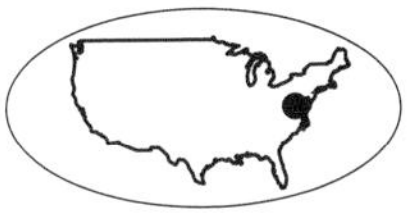

Martin R. Delany, called "the father of black nationalism," was the son of a free woman in Charles Town, West Virginia. One of his great-grandfathers had been a chief and another a prince in their native Africa. He published his own journal, *The Mystery*, in 1847, before joining Frederick Douglass (see no. 14). Co-editors of *The North Star* newspaper, Delany and Douglass printed a statement of their beliefs in 1847: "It is evident we must be our own representatives and advocates, not exclusively, but peculiarly—not distinct from, but in connection with our white friends. In the grand struggle for liberty and equality now waging, it is right and essential that there should arise in our ranks authors and editors, as well as orators."

Douglass and Delany's ideology rested on the hope that white Americans were capable of assessing African Americans honestly once they shared the same intellectual positions. They waited for a day when black men and women would lift themselves to positions equal to those of learned and respected white Americans.

Delany, whose pride and dignity became the foundation of his politics, went to Harvard Medical School in 1850 and emerged one of the most powerful antebellum influences in America. His politics shifted, as evidenced in his book, *The Condition, Elevation, Emigration and Destiny of the Colored People of the United States, Politically Considered*, which was self-published in 1853.

He claimed with great eloquence that since African Americans had not written their own history or made their own choices, their characters were still hidden. Delany, therefore, urged African Americans to move to eastern Africa where the hard work of building a free society would bring out their strongest talents.

In 1859, Delany visited Liberia and began an emigration campaign, which he abandoned when the Civil War made it possible for African Americans to achieve respect by serving equally in the armed forces. In a letter to War Secretary Edwin Stanton, Delany said "We will be ready and able to raise a regiment. . . . This is one of the measures in which the claims of the black man may be officially recognized."

Delany entered local politics after the war, only reconsidering emigration in the late 1870s. Though he and Frederick Douglass differed in their ideologies, both believed that freedom was worth all risk, whether it be here in the United States or in a new country in Africa.

**Martin R. Delany**

# 13. HENRY HIGHLAND GARNETT (1815–1882)

**Henry Highland Garnett**

Henry Garnett, whose highly influential "Address to the Slaves of the United States" united a whole generation of abolitionists, was himself born a slave in Kent County, Maryland. At ten, he escaped with his family to New Hope, Pennsylvania, and was trained as an abolitionist and a theologian in New York. His career began early. He applied to the Noyes Academy in Canaan, New Hampshire, with three other African American students, which caused such violent protest that the school shut down.

His gift for oration was discovered during his address at the American Anti-Slavery Convention in 1840. At the National Convention of Colored Citizens in Buffalo, New York, Garnett's famous address, later called Garnett's "Call to Rebellion," proved he had grown into one of the most influential speakers of his age: "Think how many tears you have poured out upon the soil which you have cultivated with unrequited toil and enriched with your blood; and then go to your lordly enslavers and tell them plainly, that you are determined to be free. . . . There is not much hope of redemption without the shedding of blood. If you must bleed, let it all come at once— rather die freemen, than live to be slaves."

His words struck cleanly into the hearts of the seventy delegates who had come from all over to address the issue of abolition. In a time of confusion and indeterminate activity, Garnett stated the price one must be willing to pay for freedom and in so doing, motivated an entire generation. Though members like Frederick Douglass (see no. 14) opposed his revolutionary tone, Garnett's words were published with David Walker's Appeal and distributed. The eloquence of his commitment urged people to follow their passion towards the final annihilation of slavery in America.

While Garnett believed that slavery was "the highest crime against God and man," he came to believe that total freedom was possible only on African land. He and his supporters were further convinced by the demoralizing passage of the 1850 Fugitive Slave Act, which helped slave owners regain possession of runaways who had escaped north.

By 1881, Garnett had embraced the idea of emigration and was made the minister of Liberia, a position he held for one year before his death in 1882. Though Garnett called for complete revolt in his most famous address, he spoke from the position of a theologian, a man devoted to the ideas of Christianity. Through the network of unified churches, people came to hear the words of men like Garnett and to commit their lives to the creation of a wholly free society.

# 14. FREDERICK DOUGLASS (1817–1895)

Frederick Douglass, perhaps the most influential man of his century, was born into great poverty. Born on an unknown date of an unknown father, Douglass lived on a Maryland plantation with his mother, who was sent to a plantation 12 miles (19 kilometers) away each day. She could occasionally walk home in time to see him to bed, but she died when Douglass was only about seven years old.

Impoverished, hungry, and parentless, Frederick struggled to survive, until the day he captured the attention of his master's daughter. Lucretia Auld had Douglass sent to Baltimore as her nephew's companion, where he learned to read and write before Lucretia's death left him without an ally. Without her influence, Douglass was sent back to the plantation and then to Baltimore to work the shipyards. There he met his future wife, Anna Murray, a free woman who used her nine years' worth of savings to pay for Douglass's successful escape to New York.

Once in New York, he was introduced to William Lloyd Garrison, and together they strengthened black resistance. Douglass was a popular speaker who mesmerized audiences with tales of his life in Maryland. He finally wrote *The Narrative of the Life of Frederick Douglass, An American Slave* to convince doubters who said he was far too eloquent and mannered to have suffered the fate he explained.

With publication came recognition, and Douglass, who was constantly in fear of slave hunters, went to England as a lecturer. The eloquence of his speeches won him immediate support, and he was encouraged to stay on indefinitely, but Douglass's commitment to African Americans still in captivity forced him to return to the United States. His English supporters were so concerned about him that they bought his freedom, allowing him to return safely to the United States.

**Frederick Douglass**

It was after his return to New York in 1847 that Douglass began publishing the famous *North Star*, named for the light that guided slaves through the night to safety. One of the most influential publications in history, *The North Star*, true to its name, united a generation of abolitionists and helped guide African Americans toward a safer future.

Along with *The North Star*, Douglass used his skills as an orator and diplomat to influence American politics. As the Civil War developed, it was Douglass who convinced President Abraham Lincoln to free all slaves immediately so that they might enlist in the Union forces. The Emancipation Proclamation was issued, and Douglass became one of the main recruiters of free African Americans in the Northern territories. At the end of the Civil War, Douglass saw a lifetime commitment rewarded with the abolition of slavery in the United States.

Until his death in 1895, Douglass continued to focus on the problems of segregation and lynchings. He joined the crusade of Mary Church Terrell (see no. 28) and Ida Wells-Barnett (see no. 27) and maintained his reputation as "the foremost leader of the nineteenth century." Also called "the father of the civil rights movement," Frederick Douglass remains a model for new generations of American heroes.

# 15. HARRIET TUBMAN (1820–1913)

**Harriet Tubman**

Harriet Tubman, perhaps the most inspirational of all abolitionists, was born into slavery in Dorchester County, Maryland. Uneducated and enslaved, it was her strong religious zeal (including visions and voices) that convinced her she would one day be free. At thirteen, after suffering a severe blow to her head while trying to intervene between a fleeing slave and his master, Harriet began to think continually about freedom.

She married a free black man named John Tubman, but he did not follow her when she finally escaped north at the age of twenty-five. She followed the north star, as hundreds did after her, to Philadelphia. She came with her fiery religious faith and a philosophy that would sustain her through unequaled acts of courage: "There was one or two things I had a right to, liberty or death; if I could not have one, I would have the other; for no man should take me alive; I should fight for my liberty as long as my strength lasted, and when the time come for me to go, the Lord would let them take me."

In Philadelphia, Tubman heard about the Underground Railroad and became its most famous "conductor." First, though she was already safe and employed in the North, she headed south and gathered up her sister Mary Ann Bowley and Mary's two children, and she led them through the secret channel of "safe houses" to Philadelphia.

This was the first of nineteen trips. Over her years on the railroad, using old spiritual songs to hide code words, carrying a gun to encourage tired travelers to continue, using opium to still crying babies, and saying prayers that called counsel from the sky, Harriet Tubman brought more than three hundred people to freedom.

Her courage was so solid that Frederick Douglass (see no. 14) wrote in a letter, "The difference between us is very marked. Most that I have done and suffered in the service of our cause has been in public. . . . You, on the other hand, have labored in a private way. I have wrought in the day—you in the night. . . . The midnight sky and the silent stars have been the witness of your devotion to freedom and of your heroism."

Tubman's heroism continued far after the Emancipation Proclamation. She tended wounded soldiers during the Civil War, acted as a spy, and helped newly freed slaves adjust to their new citizenship. She was a scout and personal assistant to General Montgomery and founder of the Harriet Tubman Home for the Aged. She raised money for the education of former slaves and participated in the New England Anti-Slavery Society with Susan B. Anthony. She died in her own retirement home of pneumonia at the age of ninety-three.

# 16. HENRY McNEAL TURNER
(1834–1915)

Henry McNeal Turner was born the son of free parents in South Carolina. Reportedly, the family's freedom was granted by British law, which honored African royalty and had freed the African prince from whom the family was descended.

Henry McNeal Turner believed in the rights of all men, and he held that they must mold the world in which they lived. He taught himself to read and write by studying with spelling, history, and law books, but his main tool was the Bible. Like many leaders before and after him, Turner found a voice that could encourage and command. That voice was nurtured by religion.

After his conversion to Christianity in 1851 and his subsequent licensing by the white Methodist Episcopal Church, Turner began to preach. During his sermons, he called on men and women to enter into all facets of society alongside white Americans, and he assured them that their voices deserved to be heard: "Thousands of white people in this country are ever and anon advising the colored people to keep out of politics. . . . If the Negro is a man in keeping with other men, why should he be less concerned about politics than anyone else? Strange too, that a number of would-be colored leaders are ignorant and debased enough to proclaim the same foolish jargon."

Turner was also an invaluable voice in favor of the reformation of Christianity. Like Absalom Jones and Richard Allen (see no. 6), he supported the idea of an African Methodist Episcopal Church. Preaching for the creation of "a black God," Turner forced people to face that even their religion glorified a white man.

Not only did Turner speak about the integration of politics and religion, he actively participated in their reformation. He organized freed slaves for the Republican Party and was elected a state legislator in 1867, although he was opposed by the new white Democratic legislators who barred him from assuming his position. Turner was a wonderful speaker, and when he brought his case forward, claiming, "I shall neither fawn nor cringe before any party, nor stoop to beg them for my rights. . . . I am here to demand my rights," he was returned to his seat, along with all other African American legislators who'd been denied their positions after election.

After only one term, Turner turned from politics to the African Methodist Episcopal Church and to the position of president of Morris Brown College in Georgia, where he continued to inspire a sense of pride and religious faith in his students.

**Henry McNeal Turner**

# 17. P. B. S. PINCHBACK (1837–1921)

**P. B. S. Pinchback**

Pinckney Benton Stewart Pinchback was denied his elected seat in the U.S. Senate in 1873, even though he was easily one of the most highly respected men of the era. He grew up in Macon, Georgia, and when his father, a white planter, died, his mother and siblings were denied any money from his estate. To help support his family, Pinchback went to work on the Mississippi riverboats.

He joined the Union Army at the start of the Civil War and was sent to recruit African American soldiers, which he did until the army's discriminatory practices led him to quit. A great idealist, Pinchback took on the issues of universal suffrage, free public schools, and civil rights for all Americans. He joined the Republican Party in Louisiana, was elected to the State Senate in 1868, and founded his newspaper, *The New Orleans Louisianian* in 1870.

Pinchback was elected lieutenant governor in 1871, and when Governor Henry Clay Warmoth was impeached, Pinchback was acting governor until he was replaced in January, 1873. In the same year, he was elected congressman-at-large and U.S. Senator. The elections were immediately contested, and Pinchback stood to defend himself: ". . . Several Senators . . . think me a very bad man. . . . I am bad because I have dared on several important occasions to have an independent opinion. I am bad because I have dared at all times to advocate and insist on exact and equal justice to all mankind."

Though his eloquence was breathtaking and his argument sound, P. B. S. Pinchback was never granted his seat in the Senate. Challenged and defeated by a senate vote of 32 to 29, P. B. S. Pinchback left politics permanently and returned to journalism. In 1875, he became chairman of the Convention of Colored Newspaper Men in Cincinnati. Speaking with great authority, he reminded African Americans of the power they could wield as a coalition: "With this force as a political element, as laborers, producers, and consumers, we are an element of strength and wealth too powerful to be ignored."

Pinchback's leadership at the convention was one of the prime ingredients in the formation of the Associated Negro Press. He continued until the end of his life to influence the greatest people working in the fields of politics and the media.

# 18. ROBERT SMALLS
(1839–1915)

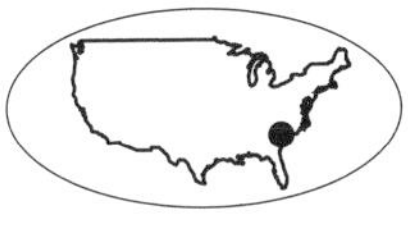

Robert Smalls, who proved himself one of the most courageous men of the Civil War, is well-known for one act of bravery against the Confederate Army.

Smalls began the war as a slave crew member on a dispatch ship called the *Planter*. An excellent sailor and devoted to the ideal of freedom, Smalls believed that risking his life and the lives of his family on the night of May 13, 1862, was the only possible chance to secure their freedom.

Officers of the *Planter* had taken their men on shore at Charleston, South Carolina, after a day of hard labor. Robert Smalls, then twenty-three years old, finding the ship's captain absent, arranged for his family and five others to sneak on board during the night. Smalls took up the captain's position and guided the *Planter* out into the channel with its eight person crew. The eyes of Confederate guards were upon him.

Smalls went on deck wearing Captain Relyea's characteristic straw hat and stood with his arms crossed over his chest as the ship glided past the guards. By the time they realized he wasn't Relyea, he had passed them and was headed straight for Union territory.

The Confederates immediately notified Morris Island, which stood in Smalls's path, but he piloted the *Planter* out of reach of the guns and prayed that Union forces wouldn't mistake him for an enemy. If they misunderstood, they might fire on the incoming ship.

Luckily for Smalls and his family, the Yankee soldiers didn't fire. Sailing carefully into the safety of Union territory, Smalls deposited the *Planter* into Union hands and joined the Union forces. Congress rewarded Smalls's amazing courage by offering him and his crew one-half of the ship's value as a reward. Smalls was also made a captain in the navy and given control of the *Planter* for the remainder of the war.

His courage became legendary, leading to the circulation of a popular story wherein two men were overheard arguing together. The first said, "Smalls, Smalls, that's all you talk about. Smalls isn't God, you know." "Sure," the second man said, "but don't forget, Smalls is young yet!"

Gaining a popular following for his support of African American education and opportunity, Robert Smalls took up politics. He was elected to the South Carolina House of Representatives, the state senate, and the U.S. Congress, where he pursued equal opportunity legislation.

**Robert Smalls**

# 19. ELIJAH McCOY (1843–1929)

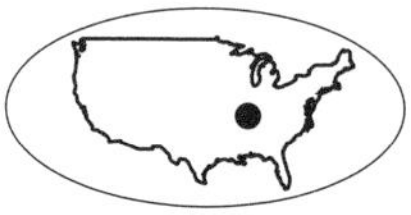

Elijah McCoy is one of the success stories of the Underground Railroad. His parents were slaves in Kentucky who took their lives into their own hands and escaped through the tunnels and tributaries that flowed toward the North Star. Arriving in Canada, they built a family of twelve children, one of whom was destined to make the name McCoy a household word.

Elijah was educated in Edinburgh, Scotland, where he became fascinated with the study of mechanical engineering. Moving from there back to the states, Elijah settled in Detroit, Michigan, in hopes of finding work. Though he was an inventive engineer, prejudice made it impossible for him to find a position except as a fireman for the Michigan Central Railroad.

This turned out to be the position that inspired him. After watching the inefficient machinery of the contemporary trains and the daily oiling of all working parts, Elijah founded the Elijah McCoy Manufacturing Company in Detroit and began working on the production of a device that would oil machinery even while the piece was still in motion. In 1872, his new "lubricator cup" received a U.S. patent and began to streamline the steam engine, saving operators valuable time and money.

**Elijah McCoy**

Though he had perfected a device that became invaluable, Elijah McCoy was not satisfied. He went to work on a variation, and perfected more than forty-two inventions that modernized machinery all over the world.

A lifetime inventor and perfectionist, Elijah McCoy remained the specialist that people trusted, and when copies were offered to prospective buyers, they would say, "I want the Real McCoy."

# 20. LEWIS HOWARD LATIMER
(1848–1928)

Lewis Howard Latimer

Howard Latimer, the creator of the Latimer Lamp, was born in Chelsea, Massachusetts, where he was allowed to go to school only until he was ten years old. When his father left the family in 1858, Lewis quit school and went to work for a legal firm, Crosby & Gould, that specialized in drafting illustrations for inventions waiting to be patented. Though Latimer was hired as an office boy, his interest in the trade led him to purchase a secondhand set of drafting tools. With books from the library and through friends in the firm, Latimer taught himself the craft of drafting.

Latimer's excellent drawings earned him the position of junior draftsman, and he was quickly promoted to chief draftsman. Then, when Latimer met Alexander Graham Bell, a friendship formed, and Bell asked for drawings of his new invention, the telephone. When Bell applied for the patent in 1876, it was Latimer's drawings that he presented.

In 1880, Latimer went to work for the United States Electric Lighting Company in Connecticut. His fascination with the detail and mechanics of drafting was the same heartfelt interest that he applied to the invention of his own lamp. After learning about the new process of electric lighting, he went to work on inventing improved filaments. He was so successful in the production of the new "Latimer Lamp" that he was then hired to oversee the building of the New York electric light plants. He was also sent to England by Maxim-Weston Electric Company to build an incandescent light division.

It was in 1884, after he'd worked with some of the age's greatest inventors, that Latimer was asked to join a small, elite group of crackerjack inventors called the Edison Pioneers. Working closely with Thomas Edison, this group came to the forefront of the contemporary age of discovery. Latimer continued with the project to the end of his life.

# 21. GEORGE WASHINGTON WILLIAMS (1849–1891)

**George Washington Williams**

George Washington Williams was a politician, journalist, historian, and fearless soldier. He began his first career by lying to the army in order to join the 6th Massachusetts Regiment at the age of fourteen. Williams was discovered, returned to civilian life, and reenlisted as a sergeant major two years later. Fearless in combat, Williams was wounded for the first time near Fort Harrison, Virginia, in 1864. He was discharged in 1865 and promptly joined the Mexican army. He resigned a year later and joined the U.S. Army's 10th Cavalry, under whose service he was wounded a second time during a campaign against the Comanche Indians of the western plains.

This time, he accepted a medical discharge and changed careers to theology. Williams graduated from the Newton Theological Institute in Massachusetts in 1874 and served as an ordained minister in Boston for a year before moving to Washington, D.C.

Williams finally chose his life's work when he began writing and publishing an influential newspaper called *The Commoner.* Men like Frederick Douglass (see no. 14) put their support behind it, and although the paper eventually went under, Williams continued to write for several other papers while he took up the study of law. In 1879, he was elected to the Ohio legislature and began to collect the details of African American lives. His collection grew to encompass two volumes he wrote. One was entitled *History of the Negro Race From 1619 to 1880.* Published in 1883, it received enormous praise for the depth of its research. Like everything Washington pursued, this book was an excellent piece of work, and it stood alone as one of the great histories of American life.

After five years, Williams published his second book, *History of the Negro Troops in the War of Rebellion.* The success of both books made Williams a popular speaker who was often invited to lecture throughout Europe. After he'd been in Belgium one year, Williams was convinced by King Leopold II to help develop the Congo Free State in Africa. Williams was so interested that he went to visit this supposed free state, which was, in fact, owned by the King. Not only were the Congolese people under the jurisdiction of King Leopold, but the workers were treated like slaves.

The conditions he found were so shocking and demoralizing that Williams wrote a letter to King Leopold II, in which he denounced the cruelty and inhumanity of the king's Congolese colony. With this and two more reports, Williams raised international interest in the Congo. He went on to research the Portuguese and British colonies in the rest of the continent.

Though he died very young, his life had been spent in the service of justice and community, and millions of lives were effected by his passion.

## 22. NAT LOVE (1854–1921)

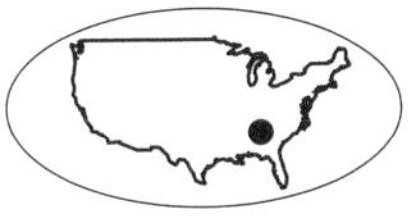

Cowboy Nat Love, also known as Deadwood Dick from his autobiography entitled *The Life and Times of Nat Love, Better Known in Cattle Country as "Deadwood Dick,"* was once a sharecropper in Tennessee. He worked hard to support his widowed mother and his sister, but when good luck came his way and granted him the winning ticket in a raffle, Love left the life of farming behind.

Selling the horse that was his prize, he gave half of the money to his mother and left for Dodge City, Kansas, where he began to live the life of legend.

There are stories about the fourteen gunshot wounds that he survived, and more tales about the skill with which he could train a horse, brand a steer, and use a gun. There are stories about his wild drinking nights with his friend Bat Masterson, and a story in which Nat Love rode his horse through a bar and ordered a couple of drinks—one for himself and one for his horse.

He was a legendary gunfighter in his youth and an exceptionally skilled one. During the 1876 Fourth of July celebration held in Deadwood, South Dakota, Love proved it by winning rifle and handgun matches, rope throws, and a bucking bronco contest. One of the many African American cowboys responsible for settling the wild western territory, Love fought Native Americans, moved with the railroad, and herded cattle for the Pete Gillinger Company in Arizona.

Even with his reputation, Love was just like any other pioneer when he left his past behind and headed west working on the railroad. Just like thousands of other bold travelers, he laid one stone on the road west. He wrote his auto-biography in 1907 and was later living in Los Angeles as a Pullman porter. By risking everything to settle new territory, he made it possible for his family to experience freedom in the United States, and for many others to follow his family's example.

**Nat Love**

# 23. TIMOTHY THOMAS FORTUNE (1856–1928)

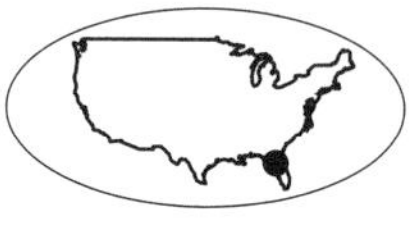

**Timothy Thomas Fortune**

T. Thomas Fortune was an influential journalist and agitator who constantly fought for the fullest implementation of the Fourteenth and Fifteenth Amendments.

Born in 1856 in Marianna, Florida, Fortune grew up while African Americans were striving hardest for the civil rights promised after the Civil War. His father had been a slave, but the Emancipation Proclamation made it possible for him to join the Florida legislature. His political influence made him a target for white Southerners who wished to cripple the Reconstruction, and Fortune's family finally moved to Jacksonville to avoid violent Ku Klux Klan threats.

T. Thomas Fortune was educated at Freedman's Bureau schools and became a printer before studying law briefly at Howard University. He moved to New York in 1879 and was hired as a printer for the *Rumor*. By 1881, the year the *Rumor* had progressed into the *Globe*, Fortune had become editor and part owner.

In 1884, Fortune bought his own newspaper, the *New York Freeman*, which became the *New York Age* in 1887. In the same year, his *Black and White: Land, Labor and Politics in the South* was published. It was a piece dedicated to Fortune's true passion: the unification of black and white forces for the civil rights—especially the right to vote—of all Americans, and particularly African Americans.

His views were further articulated during an important meeting of the National Afro-American League (NAAL) in 1890. The 147 representatives from twenty-one states heard Fortune detail the battle still in progress: "As the agitation which culminated in the abolition of African slavery in this country covered a period of fifty years, so may we expect that before the rights conferred upon us by the war amendments are fully conceded, a full century will have passed away. We have undertaken no child's play. We have undertaken a serious work which will tax and exhaust the best intelligence and energy of the race for the next century."

Fortune's newspaper became a place for the open discussion of ideals held by men like Booker T. Washington (see no. 24). Known for its militancy and its unwavering support of society's underprivileged classes, the *Age* was a powerful forum for Washington and his supporters against the separatist politics of W. E. B. Du Bois (see no. 32) and others.

Fortune remained a writer even after he sold his paper in 1907. From then until 1919, he wrote for the *Norfolk Journal*, and in 1923, he became a controversial figure once again when he became the editor of Marcus Garvey's *Negro World* (see no. 46). Garvey, called "the most dangerous enemy of the Negro people" by W .E. B. Du Bois for his "Back to Africa" policy, gave Fortune his last opportunity to shape public opinion, inspire debate, and broaden future possibilities for all Americans.

# 24. BOOKER T. WASHINGTON (1856–1915)

Booker T. Washington, one of the most politically influential men to emerge from the Reconstruction, was born into slavery, which was abolished when he was nine years old. At the end of the Civil War, his mother moved him and his family to Maiden, West Virginia. Washington began working at the salt mines and taught himself to read and write before setting out for Hampton Normal & Agricultural Institute in Virginia. An exceptional intellect, Washington rose to the top of his class and graduated with honors.

Washington showed early promise as a leader and a scholar. When the 1881 Alabama legislature decided to train black teachers at a new school in Tuskegee, the head of Hampton Normal recommended that Washington develop its programs. As the Tuskegee Institute's new president, Washington went to work building a leading institution out of an abandoned plantation in Alabama. His students were the architects and carpenters of classrooms, dormitories, a church, and a curriculum that included everything from farming to printing.

Tuskegee became the center of a self-motivation movement, and Washington's sphere of influence grew to include men like U.S. presidents William Howard Taft and Theodore Roosevelt. Washington believed that a man must take responsibility for raising his own station in life. To support Tuskegee, he befriended many wealthy businessmen and many white leaders so that he might gain their support and their financial backing. This tactic led to his reputation as an accomodationist, someone who would graciously befriend the same men who had supported slavery.

This was one of the controversial sides of Washington's ideology, though with the help of white business people, Washington made it possible for African Americans to receive the education that was critical to their survival after Reconstruction. His diplomacy was a tool for building a bridge between the separate communities, and it was the reason he was consistently invited to advise presidents and business leaders. It was also the reason that rivalries sprang up between himself and men like W. E. B. Du Bois (see no. 32).

Credited with the monumental success of Tuskegee, Washington is also known for the success of the National Negro Business League, which he founded in 1892 to support black-owned businesses. He is also remembered for the Atlanta Compromise address, which he gave in 1895, stating that "The enjoyment of all the privileges that will come to us must be the result of severe and constant struggle rather than artificial forcing." His story is detailed in his autobiography *Up From Slavery*, which was not only a bestseller in the United States but an internationally popular text.

Though his politics were hotly debated during his life and after, there is no denying that Booker T. Washington was one of the most active supporters of African American education. His ideals were based principally on the self-respect and the infinite potential of independent men and women.

**Booker T. Washington**

# 25. DR. DANIEL HALE WILLIAMS
(1848–1928)

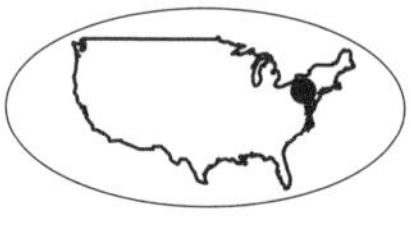

**Dr. Daniel Hale Williams**

In 1893, Dr. Daniel Hale Williams performed one of the world's medical miracles when he completed the first successful operation to repair a torn human heart. After years of dedication to the training and treatment of African Americans, Williams was catapulted into a position where other leaders, including U.S. president Grover Cleveland, were his admirers and his greatest allies in the foundation of African American hospitals.

Born in Hollidaysburg, Pennsylvania, Williams left school to apprentice with a shoemaker when he was only twelve. He attended Haire's Classical Academy in Wisconsin and apprenticed with Dr. Henry Palmer before attending Chicago Medical College. Gaining a reputation as a quick study, Williams completed Chicago Medical in only three years.

He opened his own practice, taught at Chicago Medical College, and joined the surgical staff at South Side Dispensary. Proving himself a dedicated and tireless doctor, Williams was then appointed to the Illinois State Board of Health in 1889.

Williams was extremely sensitive to the needs of African Americans and the appalling lack of facilities available both for training and treatment. He founded Provident Hospital & Training Association in 1891 and opened it to the service of all citizens and to the training of black students of medicine.

It was at Provident that Williams faced the dilemma that made him world famous. In an age where the damaged human heart was not treatable, Williams received James Cornish, a man brought to the hospital with a lethal stab wound. Without antibiotics or X rays and without any history of success, Williams managed to mend the rip in the dying man's heart. It was an invaluable evolutionary leaps for modem medicine.

President Grover Cleveland acknowledged Dr. Williams by honoring him with the position of chief surgeon at Freedman's Hospital in Washington, D.C. Williams used the influence of his new position to open a second training facility for African American doctors and nurses.

Williams continued to support the medical training and treatment of African Americans throughout his career, and by his retirement in 1926, he had helped establish more than forty new hospitals.

# 26. GRANVILLE T. WOODS (1856–1910)

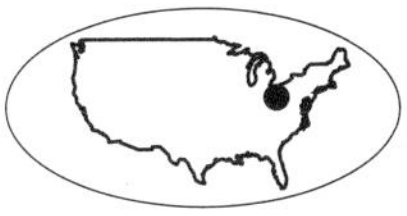

Granville T. Woods was an ingenious inventor born in Columbus, Ohio, where he was educated until the age of ten. He was then forced to leave school in order to help support his family. By the age of sixteen, Woods had already moved to Missouri, where he worked as a fireman and a railroad engineer.

Later, Woods returned to his education. He moved to New York, began working as an engineer on the steamship *Ironsides*, and studied electrical engineering. Like many great men, it was a dedication to learning that inspired Woods's greatest work. In 1884, he returned to Ohio and convinced his brother Lyates to join him in opening a new machine shop. Focusing on telephone and telegraph technology, Woods not only sold existing mechanisms but began to invent new ones.

In 1884, Woods won his first patent for a telephone transmitter so advanced that it was immediately bought by the American Bell Telephone Company in Boston. Next, he built a device that integrated the function of the telephone with that of the telegraph, and by 1887, he had won seven more patents for machines that improved communications.

Working steadily until his death. Woods patented more than sixty inventions, including a telegraph that sends messages to moving trains, the light dimmer, the electromagnetic brake, and the electrified component that allows rail cars to operate underground as subways. His inventions were highly prized by the important companies in the country. Some were bought by General Electric, others by American Bell Telephone, and still others by Westinghouse.

Woods could not be matched in the field of invention, but he took a great risk one year and accused a manager from the American Engineering Company of stealing patents. In response, the company brought a libel suit that carried on until Woods had lost nearly his entire fortune to legal fees for his defense. He died with almost nothing except the reputation as a great inventor.

**Granville T. Woods**

# 27. IDA B. WELLS-BARNETT (1862–1931)

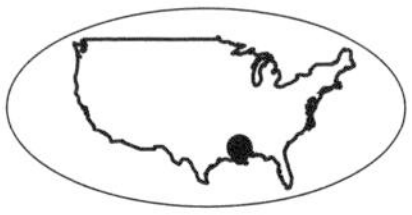

**Ida B. Wells-Barnett**

Ida Bell Wells, who dedicated her adult life to a successful anti-lynching campaign, was born a slave in Holly Springs, Mississippi. She grew up quickly after losing both her parents when she was only sixteen. Becoming the sole support to her five siblings, she lied about her age and took a job as a teacher, supporting the entire family on twenty-five dollars a month.

She moved to Missouri in 1884, continued to teach, and began writing for the *Living Way* and the *Memphis Free Speech* newspapers. When she was fired from her teaching position for protesting the poor conditions at her school, Wells took what little savings she had and bought part ownership of the *Free Speech*. Her effective reporting was responsible for increasing subscriptions by two thousand in the first nine months.

The more Wells learned, the more committed she became, and the more enemies she created. When three black men were taken from a Memphis jail and lynched, Wells reported that the men were not perpetrators of a crime, but rather successful young entrepreneurs who had begun to lure customers away from a white-owned business. Uncovering the names of the city officials who refused to condemn the lynching and those who admitted that they were in support of it, Wells caused a sensation. Her report was so damning that it convinced black citizens to refuse to use the city's expensive new streetcars as a sign of unified protest, and this boycott nearly broke the streetcar company. Wells even urged them to leave the city, and more than two thousand people moved north from Memphis in search of a just and safe society.

Ida Wells was now a celebrated journalist, and this was only the first of her investigations. She found that 1,217 African Americans had been lynched between the years of 1890 and 1900. Her famous "Red Record" detailed lynchings that occurred in three of those years. Listing the victims and the official reasons for their murders, the Red Record soon became one of the most shocking documents of American history. Here was the proof that all lynchings were not related to crimes. Of the 728 lynchings she investigated, only one-third of the victims were accused of crimes. Most of these were not even tried in a court of law.

Wells continued her investigation throughout her life. Though she was repeatedly threatened and her newspaper office was burned to the ground, she continued to research case after case from her new home in New York. She also organized women's clubs and political meetings with the help of her husband, Ferdinand Lee Barnett, whom she married in 1895. She supported the need for a national group of African American, and was an influential founder of the National Association for the Advancement of Colored People (NAACP) in 1909.

# 28. MARY CHURCH TERRELL
(1863–1954)

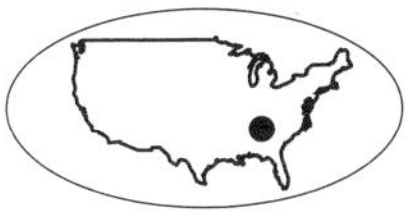

Mary Church Terrell, an extremely successful advocate of women's right—particularly black women's rights—grew up as the wealthy daughter of real estate broker Robert Church. He sent his daughter to Oberlin College, from which she graduated with a master's degree in 1888.

Mary Church Terrell was a spirited, intelligent woman who was quickly offered a position at Wilberforce University. In an age when wealthy women did not work, her father was scandalized, but no matter how he threatened, he did not stop her from accepting the position and encouraging other women to join academia: "He disinherited me . . . refused to write to me for a year because I went to Wilberforce to teach. Further, I was ridiculed and told that no man would want to marry a woman who studied higher mathematics. I said I'd take a chance and run the risk."

It was this friction that inspired Terrell to take up the issue of women's suffrage. And it was the lynching of three innocent black men in 1891 that inspired her to join the anti-lynching campaign begun by Ida B. Wells-Barnett (see no. 27).

One of the three victims had been a dear friend, and Church was compelled to contact Frederick Douglass (see no. 14) and ask his support. Together, the two of them approached U.S. president Benjamin Harrison and asked that he condemn lynching in his next address to Congress. His refusal was such a bitter disappointment that Terrell was moved to a lifetime of service against lynching and all other crimes related to racism and sexism.

She married Robert Terrell and immediately turned down a position as registrar at Oberlin College. Appointed to the Washington, D.C., Board of Education in 1895, she became the first African American woman on the board, and her influential new associates became invaluable supporters of her lifetime campaigns, which she never laid down.

Working with Susan B. Anthony and Jane Addams, Terrell helped the National American Woman Suffrage Association pass the Nineteenth Amendment. She also taught white women suffragettes to include African American women in their actions, even if it threatened their support from the South.

Terrell was a founder of the Women Wage-Earners Association, which supported black women employees. She was one of the founders of the National Association of Colored Women (NACW) and a founder of the National Association for the Advancement of Colored People (NAACP).

Dedicated to the rights of all women and the fair treatment of all men, Mary Church Terrell put pressure on the American Association of University Women to open their doors to black women, and at the age of ninety she headed a picket line that pressured restaurants into desegregation.

**Mary Church Terrell**

# 29. GEORGE WASHINGTON CARVER (1864–1943)

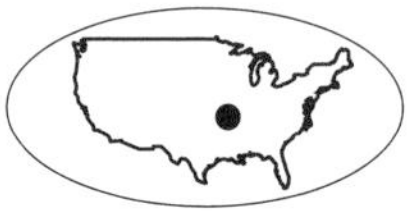

**George Washington Carver**

George Washington Carver was a scientist whose agricultural experiments at the Tuskegee Institute produced more than four hundred new products from soil-enhancing crops. He's best known for inventing byproducts of the peanut during his nearly fifty years at Tuskegee, where he was also responsible for training young African Americans to sustain themselves in the newly-reformed United States.

Born a slave in Diamond Grove, Missouri, during the Civil War, Carver and his mother were reportedly kidnapped by raiders in his youth. His mother disappeared, but a ransom was paid for Carver's return. After the Emancipation, he stayed on at the Moses and Susan Carver plantation and learned to read and write before attending school in Neosho, Missouri, and later in Kansas.

Carver's intense interest in botany led him to Highland University. He was accepted on the merits of his application but rejected when he showed up for studies and the University realized he was not white. At that time, the university did not accept African American students.

Undaunted, Carver applied to Simpson College in Iowa in 1890 and was admitted. He transferred to Iowa State University in 1891 and graduated with honors in 1894. He joined the faculty after the completion of his master's degree and remained at Iowa State until he received an intriguing letter from Booker T. Washington (see no. 24). In it, Washington said, "I can't offer you money, position or fame. . . . I offer you in their place work— hard, hard work—the task of bringing a people from degradation, poverty, and waste to full manhood."

Carver responded, "I am coming."

Carver went on to serve as director of the Agricultural Research & Experimental Station at Tuskegee Normal & Industrial Institute in Alabama. He was also an active pursuer of agricultural inventions that would replenish starved southern lands suffering from single crop nutrient depletion after generations of tobacco and cotton production. It was Carver's discovery that peanuts and other legumes could be planted for their replenishing nutrients and harvested for their superior oils, their richness in protein, and their three hundred byproducts, including peanut butter, shampoo, coffee, and face powder. One year of peanuts followed by a year of cotton not only increased the variety of production, but it increased the quality of the cotton.

He individually invented more than four hundred products made from the peanut and sweet potato alone. Carver's discoveries taught all Southerners how to maximize their land. In his own words, ". . . It has always been the one great ideal of my life to be of the greatest good to the greatest number of my people."

# 30. MATTHEW HENSON
(1866–1955)

Matthew Henson, the first man to see the North Pole, was born in Charles County, Maryland, where he lost his mother when he was only two and his father when he was eight. He went to live with an uncle in Washington, D.C., but quit school when he decided to be a sailor. Running away at the age of twelve, Henson joined Captain Child's crew on the merchant ship *Katie Hinds*. As Child's cabin boy, Henson left Baltimore and travelled around the world for six years—over the Atlantic and Pacific Oceans, into the China and Baltic Seas, and through the Straits of Magellan.

Henson became an expert at charting and navigating before returning to Washington, D.C., where he was discovered by the explorer Admiral Robert E. Peary. Peary walked into a clothing store to find Henson, an expert seaman who had retired from the sea before the age of twenty, now clerking in a clothing store. Impressed with the breadth of Henson's knowledge and experience, Peary invited him to join an expedition designed to investigate the feasibility of a canal linking the Atlantic and Pacific Oceans through Nicaragua. Henson accepted.

The Nicaragua Expedition quickly showed Peary what an invaluable associate Henson could be. When they were home again, Peary revealed that his dream had always been to be the first man to reach the North Pole; during their twenty year association, Peary and Henson undertook seven expeditions with this goal in mind.

Six times they were halted by the cruelest conditions, sometimes within a few hundred miles of their destination. Nevertheless, they began to plan the seventh expedition. Henson had taught himself to build sledges, speak the Inuit language, and master a team of dogs. When six dog teams left Crane City, Greenland, in 1908, it was with Matthew Henson in the lead.

He covered 35 miles (56 km) the first day and rose early on the second to lead Peary and a team of Inuit experts toward the top of the world. On April 6, 1909, Matthew Henson arrived at the North Pole, followed by his Inuit guides and Commander Peary.

Peary, whose progress was slow after losing several toes to frostbite, confirmed Henson's calculations, participated in about thirty hours of study, and planted the American flag.

It wasn't until 1945 that Henson received the Navy Medal from Congress, and not until 1961 that a plaque was erected in his honor at the State House at Annapolis, Maryland. In 1988, Henson's remains were moved to Arlington National Cemetery, where he was buried with full honors next to Robert Peary.

**Matthew Henson**

# 31. MADAME C. J. WALKER
(1867–1919)

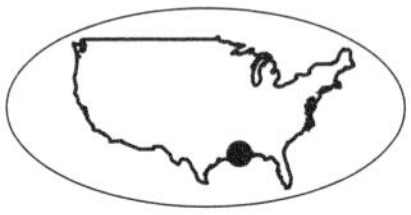

**Madame C. J. Walker**

Sarah Breedlove was a woman who turned her inventive mind and excellent business sense into a million dollar company, improving not only the quality of her own life but also that of many African Americans.

Breedlove"s parents were both recently freed slaves who died when she was only five. She then left the Louisiana plantation where she was born and lived with her sister until marrying a man named McWilliams when she was fourteen. She lost him as well, to a lynch mob, when she was only twenty. Left alone to raise her young daughter A'lelia, she went to work as a washerwoman and sacrificed her health to take good care of her child. Poverty and bad nutrition, combined with traditional "wrap and twist" hair straightening methods, made her hair begin to thin.

Breedlove began experimenting with methods to stop hair loss and one night had a dream in which an old man gave her the ingredients for a potion that not only stopped balding, but quickened regrowth. By the time she met her second husband, the newspaperman C. J. Walker, Sarah Breedlove and her relatives were already filling jars with her Wonderful Hair Grower and selling them. It was Walker who taught her the advertising and mail order techniques that changed her small business into a million dollar success.

Madame C. J. Walker went on to fashion hair care products particularly designed for black hair. She developed the hot comb and promoted the idea that beauty was derived from cleanliness and not from racial qualities. She opened her first beauty school, the Leiia College, in Pittsburgh in 1908, and she managed a staff of door-to-door agents who began to earn up to one thousand dollars a day in commissions. By 1919, twenty-five thousand agents worked for her. They taught women how to take pride in their beautiful hair and skin while encouraging them to start their own beauty shops.

Walker's success allowed her to send A'lelia to Knoxville College and to begin focusing on her own education. With independent tutors, Madame Walker concentrated for the first time on the luxuries of a formal education. Her respect for higher learning would ultimately lead her to donate money to several institutions and leaders, including Tuskegee Institute and Frederick Douglass (see no. 14).

Throughout her life, Walker asserted that if a woman could run her own business, she could certainly manage her own life. She put hundreds of women to work in her company and in their own beauty shops. Walker made sure that her success promoted the success of all women looking for means to manage their own lives. Her example taught women how to pursue business for themselves, appreciate their own beauty, and take responsibility for their own education.

# 32. W. E. B. DU BOIS (1868–1963)

William Edward Burghardt Du Bois was born in Great Barrington, Massachusetts. Through founding the Niagara Movement and *Crisis* magazine and motivating innumerable leaders, Du Bois became an influential role model for generations of African Americans. He was the first black man to graduate from Harvard with a Ph.D. in Social Sciences, and his doctoral dissertation, *The Suppression of the African Slave Trade*, became his first book, published in 1896.

Du Bois accepted a position as professor of history and economics at Atlanta University, and while there he helped in the formation of the first formal black academic committee, the American Negro Academy. His eloquent and educational essays were published in a famous collection called *The Souls of Black Folk*, where Du Bois covered numerous issues related to race, including his negative opinion of Booker T. Washington's tactics of appeasement (see no. 24) in the overwhelmingly white world of education and economics. It was also during his time at Atlanta that Du Bois and others formed the Niagara Movement (1905), an organization in direct opposition to Booker T. Washington's Tuskegee Movement. The Niagara Movement was based on such principles as a militant response to all racial discrimination, the idea of complete equality between races, and the education of what Du Bois called "a talented tenth" of the Negro population who could then lead the entire population toward "self-realization and its highest cultural possibilities." It was the Niagara Movement that grew into perhaps the most influential African American coalition in history, the National Association for the Advancement of Colored People (NAACP).

**W. E. B. Du Bois**

Though the conflicting ideas of Du Bois and Washington split African American communities into separate factions, they also managed to inspire a debate that drove people to envision new futures for African Americans.

And neither man stopped there. Du Bois began to publish the monthly magazine *Crisis*, which highlighted the issues and writings of black leaders. In 1910, he left Atlanta to lead the NAACP as director of research and publicity, and *Crisis* grew into a forum for the ideas of African American writers and artists who would later be associated with the Harlem Renaissance, including Langston Hughes (see no. 64), Marian Anderson (see no. 63), and Arna Bontemps.

He was a consistently fine writer whose works include *Black Reconstruction* and *The World and Africa*. He cofounded the Pan-African Congress in 1919, and he later became a devoted peace activist who chaired the Peace Information Center against the proliferation of atomic weapons.

Investigated and indicted for his relationship to a "foreign agent" in 1951, Du Bois's passport was denied. He was shunned by many of his associates and unable to continue much of his work until 1958, when the U.S. Supreme Court struck down the validity of the court's original statute. Du Bois toured Asia, Europe and the Soviet Union before moving to Ghana on President Kwame Nkrumah's invitation, where he began to edit the *Encyclopedia Africana*. He remained in Ghana until his death.

# 33. JOHN HOPE
(1868–1936)

John Hope

John Hope's own words are perhaps the most telling statement of his life's work and his character: "If we are not striving for equality, in heaven's name for what are we living? I regard it as cowardly and dishonest for any of our colored men to tell white people or colored people that we are not struggling for equality. . . . Yes, my friend, I want equality. Nothing less. . . . If equality, political, economic, and social, is the boon of other men in this great country of ours, then equality, political, economic, and social, is what we demand. . . . Rise, Brothers! Come let us possess this land. Never say: 'Let well enough alone.' Cease to console yourselves with adages that numb the moral sense. Be discontented. Be dissatisfied."

John Hope's statement is particularly striking when it is understood against the background of his situation. This speech was made in Nashville in 1906 and in response to Booker T. Washington's Atlanta Compromise address (see no. 24). John Hope was the president of Atlanta Baptist College at the time, and as such, a very visible figure. In great opposition to Washington and all the powerful white supporters of his college, he was also a great friend of W. E. B. DuBois (see no. 32).

Hope was born in Augusta, Georgia. He'd graduated with a B.A. from Brown University in 1894 and taught at Atlanta Baptist College for eight years before he became president there. When he stood up as president and opposed the compromises of Washington and his supporters, John Hope was declaring publicly that he held equality above all other treasures—above even the security of his career.

That courage made him a great ally to Du Bois and the other influential members of the Niagara Movement. It also made him a powerful force in the field of education. Asserting that African Americans must enter into higher education, Hope helped shape the policies of the nation's schools by presiding over both Atlanta Baptist College and Atlanta University—an affiliate school that served both men and women. He also presided over both the National Association of Teachers of Colored Schools and the Association for the Study of Negro Life & History.

A man held in the highest esteem, John Hope finished his life in the service of higher learning after a lifetime of holding his peers to the ideal of equality.

# 34. SCOTT JOPLIN
(1868–1917)

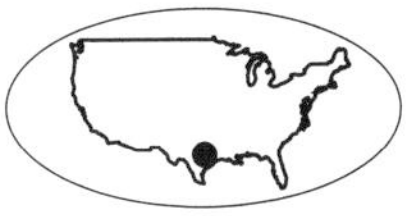

Scott Joplin, considered "the King of Ragtime," was born in Texarcana, Texas, where he taught himself to play piano in the houses where his mother worked as a maid. News of his talent spread through the city, and soon a German music teacher picked Joplin up as a student and taught him the formalities of music.

When Joplin's mother died, he began to travel as a musician, taking note of emerging musical styles and finding a particular interest in the syncopated rhythms of ragtime. Based on old slave tunes, ragtime combined their soulful melodies with varied rhythm patterns, producing a fast, even sound that became the basis of a new dance craze. "Ragging the melody," which began on New Orleans riverboats, swept through urban dance halls, and when Scott Joplin played it, ragtime became the signature of a generation.

Joplin moved to St. Louis in 1895 and began playing his brand of ragtime at Honest John Turpin's Silver Dollar Saloon. He then moved to Sedalia, where he took classes in music theory from George R. Smith College. At night, he practiced his own style at the Maple Leaf Club. He then began to publish his music.

In 1899, Joplin's "Oriental Rags" was published, but his next piece, the famous "Maple Leaf Rag" was rejected by two publishers before music dealer John Stark printed it. It sold more than one million copies. The most popular piece of sheet music in publication at the time, the "Maple Leaf Rag" made ragtime an international sensation.

As ragtime's popularity soared and Joplin's simpler rags became popular, he became entranced with a new form. Interested in achieving the musical excellence of European classics, Joplin followed his passion for artistic complexity and began writing opera. His first. *The Guest of Honor*, was not well received. Joplin began work on the next, a folk opera in honor of his mother. *Treemonisha* was such a complex and unique piece of music that Joplin could not find a producer. Deciding to risk everything, he produced the piece himself with complete faith. He then watched it close almost immediately. Joplin's audience, unimpressed and disappointed, rejected his opera at the same time that his ragtime was being replaced by a new form called jazz.

Joplin never recovered from the disappointment of *Treemonisha's* failure. Committed to Manhattan State Hospital in 1916, Joplin died that spring without realizing that his music would be revived in the last half of the twentieth century. "The Entertainer" became the chosen theme song for the Academy Award-winning movie *The Sting*, and *Treemonisha* was finally produced on Broadway in the 1970s, where it delighted contemporary audiences. Joplin remains forever and always "the King of Ragtime."

**Scott Joplin**

# 35. ROBERT ABBOTT
(1870–1940)

**Robert Abbott**

Robert Abbott, the founder and editor of *The Chicago Defender*, was raised in Georgia by his mother and his stepfather, a man who had such a positive influence on Abbott that he took his surname, Sengstacke, as his middle name. It was in Sengstacke's Georgian newspaper office that Abbott learned the printing trade. He then left for Chicago, where he attended Hampton Institute and Kent College of Law.

After graduation, Abbott tried to found a practice and ended up moving to the Midwest. After working for five years, he returned to Chicago in 1903. In 1905, he reportedly invested his entire savings, a total of 25 cents, into the first edition of *The Chicago Defender*. The first issue was a four-page document produced at a desk in his landlady's kitchen and sold door-to-door for two cents each. These were the humble beginnings of one of the United States' influential black newspapers.

Dedicated to increasing the migration of African Americans to the comparatively liberal North, *The Defender* was one of the few voices speaking honestly on black issues and educating people about lynchings, the coming machination of farming in the South, and the improved standard of living for African Americans in the industrialized North.

*The Chicago Defender* was a strong supporter of the NAACP and claimed the newspaper's goals were the same as the NAACP's: manhood suffrage, an end to discrimination in public accommodations, the right to socialize with all willing to socialize with them, equality under the law, and education for all children.

To these ends, Abbott published some of the best writers and thinkers on the subjects of concern to black America. Though *The Defender* was sometimes banned in areas for its militancy, Abbott often supported his position with dramatic exposes on the extremity of racism, the violence, and the dire economic circumstances experienced by African Americans in both the South and the North.

Outside the newspaper, Abbott was a great activist. Serving on the Chicago Commission of Race Relations, he worked for the desegregation of neighborhoods and supported political candidates who fought for the inclusion of African Americans in President Franklin Roosevelt's New Deal policies.

# 36. JAMES WELDON JOHNSON
(1871–1938)

James Weldon Johnson, writer, musician, and member of the NAACP, was born in Jacksonville, Florida. James attended Atlanta University, from which he graduated in 1894, before returning to Jacksonville, where he took the position of principal of the Stanton School until 1901.

In that year, he and his talented brother J. Rosamond Johnson moved to New York City, where they became musical collaborators on songs like "Since You Went Away" and "Lift Every Voice and Sing." They wrote for the stage with Robert Cole and saw their pieces performed on Broadway.

All of this was a precursor to Johnson's involvement in the Harlem Renaissance, which brought elements of black culture to the forefront of American culture. Along with icons Langston Hughes (see no. 64), Marian Anderson (see no. 63), Claude McKay (see no. 47), and others who were writing and performing in Harlem, James Weldon Johnson became a spokesperson for the African American experience. He was one of the artists aware of the economic and social problems of post-war America at a time when the United States was celebrating peace with a lot of patriotism. With new pride and articulate voices, the writers of the Renaissance demanded the respect their obvious artistry deserved.

In 1906, Johnson was President Theodore Roosevelt's choice for U.S. consul in Venezuela, and in 1909, he was transferred to Nicaragua. In 1912, Johnson's career as an influential novelist began with the publication of *The Autobiography of an Ex-Colored Man*, in which he detailed the life of a black man passing for white. In 1913, he became editor for the *New York Age*, and in 1916, he began to use his diplomatic experience to help the NAACP. He became the agency's secretary and oversaw the organization of new branches throughout the nation, while focusing further attention on the powerful anti-lynching campaign headed by his associate Ida B. Wells-Barnett (see no. 27).

With the dawn of the Harlem Renaissance, which made Harlem, New York, one of the world's exciting cultural centers of the 1920s and 30s, Johnson published extensively. *The Book of American Negro Spirituals* was published in 1925, its sequel in 1926, and *God's Trombones, Seven Negro Sermons in Verse*, *Black Manhattan*, and *Negro American, What Now?* all before 1935.

One of the first African Americans to use aesthetics to further diplomatic relations between races, Johnson was influential in inspiring this nation to finally destroy its dividing lines: "The stereotype is that the Negro is nothing more than a beggar at the gate of the nation, waiting to be thrown crumbs of civilization. Through his artistic efforts the Negro is smashing this immemorial stereotype faster than he has ever done through any other method he has been able to use. He is making it realized that he is the possessor of a wealth of natural endowments and that he has long been a generous giver to America."

**James Weldon Johnson**

# 37. PAUL LAURENCE DUNBAR
(1872–1906)

**Paul Laurence Dunbar**

Paul Laurence Dunbar, one of the first poets to effectively employ "black dialect" as a tool in poetry, was born to former slaves in Dayton, Ohio. In school in Dayton, he joined the literary society and served on the staff of the school newspaper.

In 1893, he published his first poetry collection entitled *Oak and Ivy*. His second, *Majors and Minors* (1895), was followed by the internationally recognized collection *Lyrics of Lowly Life* (1896). With an introduction by the esteemed critic William Dean Howells, who praised Dunbar for being "the only man of pure African blood and of American civilization to feel the Negro life aesthetically and express it lyrically," *Lyrics of a Lowly Life* became the definitive poetic text on the black experience.

Dunbar's acceptance into the literary world was one that lost him support in the African American community. Viewed as an accommodationist more like Booker T. Washington (see no. 24) than W. E. B. Du Bois (see no. 32), Dunbar was accused of creating characters that were stereotyped by their foolish, fun-loving simplicity. He was accused of avoiding subjects like Jim Crow laws and the rise in lynchings in his short story collections, *Folks From Dixie* (1898), *In Old Plantation Days* (1903), and *The Heart of Happy Hollow* (1904). But he was also given credit for being one of the only poets who honestly simulated African American speech patterns in his work, bringing an artistic representation of black culture to his broad national audience.

Because he was extremely popular with white readers, Dunbar's voice was valuable when applied to social criticism. He wrote about African American heroes in "The Colored Soldiers" and "Harriet Beecher Stowe," and he acknowledged the pain of racism in "Sympathy," from which the phrase "I know why the caged bird sings" was extracted for the title of Maya Angelou's autobiography (see no. 89).

In 1898, when the success of the industrialized North was feeding a debate between blacks and whites over education, Dunbar urged African Americans to remember the rewards of classical learning. He stated that "People are taking it for granted that the Negro ought not to work with his head. And it is so easy for these people among whom we are living to believe this." He went on to state that "though men need not bury their heads permanently in scholarly works, they must temper their new passion for industry with a passion for art, science, and idealism. He urged them to remember the difference between utilitarianism and beauty."

His own artistic career ended when Dunbar succumbed to tuberculosis at age thirty-three.

# 38. WILLIAM M. TROTTER
(1872–1934)

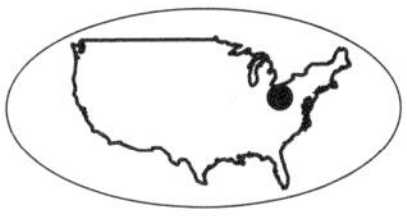

William Trotter, militant member of the Niagara Movement and founder of *The Boston Guardian*, was born in Chillicothe, Ohio, but raised in Boston. He went to an all-white high school before attending Harvard and gaining admittance to the prestigious Phi Beta Kappa fraternity. He graduated Harvard in 1894 and took a job in real estate after his father's example. In 1899, Trotter quit the company and opened his own, which he gave up in 1901 to found *The Boston Guardian*, which grew into the most militant African American publication of its age.

Trotter's *Guardian* was used as a major tool against appeasement. Demanding equality without compromise, he filled its pages with attacks on the African Americans who worked closely with white Americans to slowly alter racist policies. He was a combatant, a man willing to enter confrontations and disrupt powerful conferences in order to demand immediate and complete equality.

He was known for acts such as halting a church meeting speech by Booker T. Washington (see no. 24) in 1903. He spent thirty days in jail, along with fellow protester Greenville Martin, because he had refused to desist. He was a passionate voice against U.S. president Woodrow Wilson's segregation of Washington departments and a man who would not join the National Association for Advancement of Colored People, after being very active in the preceding Niagara Movement, because he did not trust the white members of the alliance.

Along with the publication of the leftist *Guardian*, Trotter was responsible for the founding of the National Equal Rights League, which was supported by an entirely black membership and stood on a platform of more militant demands.

Though Trotter moved few mountains with his powerful protests and his impassioned demands, he was an important influence on the growing power of the black press in the United States, and a fearless voice against even the subtlest forms of racism.

In 1934, Trotter apparently leapt to his death from the roof of his Boston boarding-house. He died a lonely man after spending much of his life in brilliant opposition to society's bias. His actions were always in answer to a growing public demand for greater civil rights.

**William M. Trotter**

# 39. WILLIAM CHRISTOPHER HANDY (1873–1958)

W. C. Handy, often credited with fathering popular blues music, was first told by his mother that he would be a musician; she said his big ears were the source of his musical ability. In his home town of Florence, Alabama, Handy learned to play everything from harmonicas and clay jugs to combs and broom handles.

It was in 1909 that Handy wrote his first big hit. Beginning as an election campaign song for Memphis mayor Edward Crump, the famous "Memphis Blues" became a national sensation. Handy did not receive the financial benefit, but he went on to write "St. Louis Blues" in 1914, which became an even bigger hit. It was the beginning of a brand new phase in music. The blues, based on the old black spirituals, folk ballads and working man's songs, made melancholy by flatted thirds and sevenths, became one of the nation's favorite musical modes of expression.

In his tours throughout the nation, Handy began distributing the outlawed *Chicago Defender*, published by radical civil rights activist William Trotter (see no. 38). With great risk to himself, Handy had decided to help his listeners make the move to the North away from widespread racial discrimination of the South. Some believe that when he wrote, "I hate to see the evening sun go down," he referred to the danger of traveling through small Southern towns where he was not known by his face or his music but by the color of his skin alone.

**William Christopher Handy**

In 1918, after listening to the regional music styles of the nation, Handy began chronicling what he heard, and he and his partner, Harry Pace, opened the Pace and Handy Music Company. Along with "Beale St. Blues" in 1919, Handy went on to write a number of pieces that inspire contemporary musicians still—"A Good Man is Hard to Find" and "Careless Love" among them.

Pace and Handy flourished throughout the turbulent war years, and though Handy eventually went blind in 1943, he continued to carve a place for his music, and the music of all African Americans. Blues music, still one of the most popular musical art forms, continues to be a credit to his innovation and that of African American musicians around the nation.

# 40. ARTHUR SCHOMBURG
(1874–1938)

Arthur Schomburg

Arthur Schomburg, who's been called "the Sherlock Holmes of Black History" for the extensive research that went into his collection of texts and images, was born in San Juan, Puerto Rico. It was there that he developed an intense interest in the history of fellow African Americans. After collecting for years, he carried his wide body of historical documentation from the Virgin Islands, where he attended St. Thomas College, to the United States in 1891.

Schomburg worked in a law office while collecting more documents but left the company in 1906 to join the Bankers Trust Company. Staying until his retirement in 1929, Schomburg continued his research while collaborating with some of the era's greatest African American leaders.

In 1911, Schomburg and John E. Brace founded the Negro Society for Historical Research, and in 1922, Schomburg was made president of the American Negro Academy, the first American group of African American intellectuals.

Schomburg's interest in history was not just for the sake of knowledge but for the sake of African American identity and pride. His ideas were eloquently outlined in an essay published in 1925 entitled "The Negro Digs Up His Past," in which he stated the theories proved by history but ignored: that the Negro has actively pursued freedom and advancement; that brilliant African American thinkers have been treated as exceptions, and the race has not been credited with their achievements; and that racially, Negroes achieved a credible, scientifically successful society without the influence of white leaders.

In order to make these assertions known, Schomburg felt that history was a tool to be used skillfully. His collection, made up of thousands of documents and artifacts, was exceptional. In 1925, the New York Public Library dedicated a branch to Negro literature and history, and in 1926, more than five thousand items were bought by the Carnegie Corporation and donated to the branch.

When Schomburg retired, Fisk University made him curator of their Negro collection, until 1932, when the Carnegie Corporation made it possible for the New York Public Library to hire him as curator at the Division of Negro Literature, History, and Prints, where his collection was still housed.

Schomburg continued to add to the collection, and after his death, its name was changed to the Schomburg Center for Research in Black Culture, where there are now more than five million artifacts, photos, and manuscripts, and more than one-hundred thousand books on African American history.

# 41. MARY McLEOD BETHUNE
(1875–1955)

Mary McLeod Bethune, founder of the Daytona Normal and Industrial School, was born the fifteenth child, but the first free child, of her family in Mayesville, South Carolina. From the beginning, she was a fiercely hard worker, picking cotton, washing and ironing, and walking 5 miles (8 km) to school each day. It was her job to bring home everything she learned and teach it to her brothers and sisters. This may have been the single most effective training Mary McLeod Bethune had in the value of education.

Mary attended Scotia Seminary on a scholarship, but she graduated from Moody Bible Institute in Chicago. In 1904, she and her new husband, teacher Albertus Bethune, moved to Daytona, Florida, and Mary began to plan the school she would one day build.

In 1904, on a piece of land used mainly for dumping, Bethune put down a five dollar payment and promised to buy the land outright for two hundred dollars in two years' time. She then went to work educating five little girls and her own son Albert. By the time the bill was due on the land, Bethune had 250 students. The Daytona Normal and Industrial School, which later joined the coeducational Cookman Institute to form the Bethune-Cookman College, was firmly established.

Dedicated to education and civil rights, and specifically that of African American women, Bethune gave a lifetime to the formation and organization of groups like the powerful National Council of Negro Women (1935) and the National Youth Administration (NYA), which U.S. president Franklin Roosevelt asked her to advise as the Director of Negro Affairs. She was also a member of the National Association of Colored Women (NACW), which she aligned with the primarily white International Council of Women.

**Mary McLeod Bethune**

Working ultimately with five United States presidents, Bethune's leadership became a respected and highly prized asset. She made sure the Women's Army Auxiliary Corps allotted 10 percent of its officer candidate spaces to blacks. She befriended both Franklin and Eleanor Roosevelt and was able to secure federal funding for vocational training and jobs for African American youth. She secured funds for black housing projects in Florida, forced John Hopkins Hospital to hire African American doctors, and appealed to Franklin Roosevelt on behalf of Jewish victims during their persecution in World War II.

Throughout her life, Bethune worked wholeheartedly for the increased power of African Americans in United States policy and served those ends by offering opportunity, education, and dignity.

# 42. GARRETT MORGAN
(1875–1963)

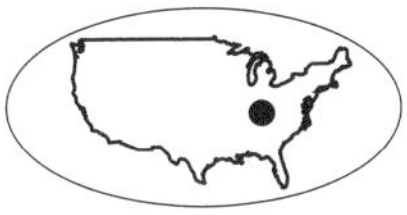

Garrett Morgan, inventor of many modem life savers, including the gas mask and the three-way stoplight, was born in Paris, Kentucky, on a farm that he left at the age of fourteen. From Kentucky, he headed north to Cincinnati, Ohio, where he found work as a handyman. He stayed in Cincinnati for six years, working with a tutor to improve his grammar, and moved on to Cleveland in 1895.

In Cleveland, Morgan began to focus on the building of businesses. He took a job as a sewing machine adjuster but only long enough to learn the business and open his own sewing machine repair shop. His next venture, a tailor shop, eventually grew to employ thirty-two workers.

Through trying to improve business, Morgan came across some of his finest inventions. While trying to formulate a polish for sewing needles, he discovered a way to straighten hair. His new Morgan Hair Refining Company became a huge financial success.

It's been said that since he was the first man in Cincinnati to own his own car, it's possibly no surprise that he was also the first to invent the three-way stoplight.

These inventions, though financially rewarding, were not equal to the one he perfected in 1916 that would save thousands of lives—the gas mask. On July 25, Morgan was summoned for what became the most important trial run for this new invention. As thirty-two workers lay buried in a tunnel below Lake Erie, where a huge explosion had trapped them in a cell with poison gas, Morgan, his brother Frank, and two volunteers donned the masks that had won Morgan the grand prize at the New York Safety and Sanitation Fair.

Believing they had a twenty minute air supply, Morgan and the others went into the tunnel, found the unconscious workers of the Cleveland Waterworks Company, and pulled them one by one to their families and associates waiting breathlessly outside the tunnel.

Every fire department in the country began placing orders for Morgan's gas masks, until it was discovered that Morgan was black. When orders slowed down, Morgan hired a white man to demonstrate the device, as if he were the inventor, while Morgan assisted.

In 1917, when the United States entered World War I, it was Morgan's improved gas masks that protected the American soldiers from the enemy's poisonous chemical weapons.

Though racist attitudes never managed to defeat him, Morgan was dedicated to the idea that African Americans should no longer be forced to endure them. He joined the NAACP, founded the *Cleveland Call* newspaper to improve reporting on African American issues, and ran for Cleveland's City Council in 1931. Though he did not win, he became another symbol of the growing success of African Americans.

**Garrett Morgan**

# 43. CARTER GODWIN WOODSON (1875–1950)

**Carter Godwin Woodson**

Carter Woodson, "the Father of Negro History" who employed scientific methods in his research of African American roots, was born the first of nine children in New Canton, Virginia. Postponing his education so that he could help support his family, Woodson did not attend school until he was twenty years old. Self-educated, he took one year to earn a high school degree before heading to Berea College in Kentucky. He completed his first B.A. in 1903 and received his second, plus an M.A., from the University of Chicago in 1908, after taking time off to travel to Europe, Asia, and Africa. Completing his Ph.D. at Harvard in 1912, Woodson emerged as a teacher, a historian, and a brilliant activist determined to inspire African Americans to embrace and celebrate their own history.

Woodson's greatest achievement was the formation of a "black historiography," a body of history proven by the employment of scientific methods and procedures. In his many published works, including *The Education of the Negro Prior to 1861* (1915), *A Century of Negro Migration* (1918), *The History of the Negro Church* (1921), and *The African Background Outlined* (1936), Woodson detailed the history of which he was proud, and he inspired his contemporaries to embrace it with the same pride. Collecting historical documents and publishing them in anthologies, Woodson brought history to life: *Negro Orators and Their Orations* (1925), *The Mind of the Negro as Reflected in Letters Written During the Crisis, 1800-1860* (1926), *The Miseducation of the Negro* (1933) and *African Heroes and Heroines* (1939).

He was also an active organizer. He founded the Association for the Study of Negro Life & History in 1915 and began to publish the *Journal of Negro History* in 1916. Interested in opening new opportunities for education, Woodson established Negro History Week (which has evolved into Black History Month) in 1926. He began to publish the *Negro History Bulletin* in 1937 as a tool for educators teaching black history to primary and secondary school children.

Interested in factual details and the inspirational quality of history, Woodson left many lessons for contemporary educators and activists: "We have a wonderful history behind us. . . . It reads like the history of people in an heroic age. . . . If you read the history of Africa, the history of your ancestors—people of whom you should feel proud—you will realize that they have a history that is worthwhile. They have traditions that have value of which you can boast and upon which you can base a claim for the right to share in the blessings of democracy."

# 44. JACK JOHNSON
(1878–1946)

Jack Johnson, the first black heavyweight champion of the world, was born in Galveston, Texas, where he attended school until the fifth grade. Leaving home soon after, Johnson took odd jobs in stables and on the docks, slowly building a reputation as a fighter. By the age of eighteen, he was already well-respected for "barnstorming his way through the United States," as Columbus Salley wrote.

In 1887, Johnson went professional. He married his childhood love, Mary Austin. He was an unavoidable force in the white-dominated world of professional boxing. In 1906, Johnson was granted a match with Bob Fitzsimmons, the former heavyweight champion of the world. In a finish that rocked the boxing world, Fitzsimmons went down and the fight ended in an unprecedented knockout. Johnson soon sought a match with the then-current champion, James Jeffries. Jeffries refused to fight Johnson because he was a black man and retired undefeated soon after. Jeffries's successor, Tommy Burns, accepted Johnson's challenge and went into the ring with him on December 26, 1908, in Australia. The world watched breathlessly as Johnson took him down too, proving himself the heavyweight champion of the world.

Known for his flashy style and his womanizing, Johnson became a thorn in the side of many white fans and fighters alike. Many wanted to see him lose badly, and when James Jeffries announced that he would come out of retirement in 1910, they thought they'd get the chance.

Jeffries made a public announcement that clearly defined the racial connotations of the competition: "I fully realize what depends upon me and won't disappoint the public. That portion of the white race which is looking to me to defend its athletic supremacy may feel assured that I am fit to do my very best. I'll win as quickly as I can."

Jeffries's statement only made it sweeter when he hit the mat in the fifteenth round. Unfortunately, a small part of the nation couldn't accept that their champion was unequal to Johnson. Race riots erupted around the nation, and both black and white citizens lost their lives before the rioters were subdued.

Johnson remained the undefeated champion until 1915, when Jess Willard, nicknamed "the White Hope," won the title in the twenty-sixth round of a match in Havana, Cuba.

Though there was some dispute over the knockout that ended Johnson's career, there was no question that Johnson had inspired pride in the world of African American athletics and paved the way for such upcoming national heroes as Muhammad Ali (see no. 100) and Joe Louis. Jack Johnson died in Raleigh, North Carolina, after receiving lethal injuries in a car racing crash.

**Jack Johnson**

# 45. OSCAR MICHEAUX (1884–1951)

**Oscar Micheaux**

Oscar Micheaux was the most influential filmmaker to contradict Hollywood's depictions of African Americans. He was born into a family of thirteen siblings in Cairo, Illinois, and left home as a young teenager. Micheaux took a number of odd jobs before finally becoming a Pullman porter who traveled extensively throughout the nation, becoming ever more infatuated with the West. He settled a homestead in South Dakota in 1904 and founded his own publishing company so that he could release his own novels about African American experiences in the West. His first book, *The Conquest: The Story of a Negro Pioneer*, was published in 1913 and promoted by Micheaux himself, who traveled in Western costume, selling his books directly to African American communities. Selling them by hand, Micheaux built a national audience for each of his ten novels.

When he was approached by a production company interested in adapting his novel *The Homesteader* to the screen, Micheaux demanded that he be allowed to direct it. His demands were rejected, and Micheaux refused the project, but he was inspired by the idea. He founded the Oscar MicheauxCorporation, an independent film company in New York, and set to work in the production of nonracist representations of African Americans in film.

Focusing on middle-class characters, African Americans who were neither impoverished nor miserable, Micheaux created more than thirty-five films, including *Homesteader* (1919), *Within Our Gates, The Brute, Symbol of the Unconquered* (1920), *Son of Satan* (1922) *Harlem After Midnight* (1934) and *God's Stepchildren* (1937).

Determined to counteract Hollywood's stereotypical cardboard characterizations of African Americans, Micheaux focused on a segment of the population engrossed in the middle-class ideals of American society. Though he is sometimes criticized for evading the issues of poverty and racial discrimination, his ideal was to create a new characterization that did not portray African Americans as devoted servants or African savages. To these ends, Micheaux was the first to create an influential and intelligent body of film that treated black Americans simply as Americans.

# 46. MARCUS GARVEY
(1887–1940)

Marcus Garvey was considered a brilliant black nationalist by many—and a dangerous enemy by W. E. B. Du Bois (see no. 32) and other African American intellectuals. He was born the youngest of eleven children in St. Ann's Bay, Jamaica, where he quit school early and became a printer's apprentice. In 1907, he lost his job after helping to organize a company strike. First, he moved to Costa Rica, where he worked on a banana plantation. He then went to Panama, where he worked for a newspaper, and to London, where he met Duse Mohammed Ali and other Africans organizing for independence. He read the inspirational works of men like Booker T. Washington (see no. 24) and embraced the idea that he was born to lead the black race out of degradation and poverty.

He returned to Jamaica in 1914 and founded the Universal Negro Improvement Association & African Communities League (UNIA). With the desire to make the UNIA an African association that could protect blacks all over the world, Garvey built a school on the model of Washington's Tuskegee Institute. Although it was unsuccessful, the attempt gained Garvey an invitation to visit the original university.

Coming to the United States in 1915, four months after Washington's death, Garvey met with civil rights leaders of the day while recruiting members for the UNIA. Though he disagreed hotly with the intellectual community headed by Du Bois, Garvey struck a chord with the rest of the American public.

By 1919, Garvey had opened branches of the UNIA in thirty cities and had enticed more than two million members. He had begun to publish *The Negro World*, which went out weekly to the West Indies, Latin America, Africa. and the United States. He had raised money to support the concept of an African nation led by the purest African men and had founded the Black Star Line, a three-ship company with only African American stockholders. The Black Star Line was not only a financial venture but a way to bring African Americans back to "the African Motherland."

Garvey's popularity continued to soar as he opened the Negro Factories Corporation, which gave financial and technical assistance to small businesses, and in August 1920, he held a month-long convention/festival in Harlem called the First International Convention of the Negro Peoples of the World. The delegates of the convention were so enthused that they voted to build a free republic of Africa. Garvey was to be its leader.

Before he could realize his ideal, Garvey's Black Star Line went bankrupt, and he himself was tried for mail fraud. Convicted, Garvey went to jail in 1925, serving two years before U.S. president Calvin Coolidge ordered him deported to Jamaica.

Garvey went to London in 1935 and lived there until a stroke took his life in 1940.

**Marcus Garvey**

# 47. CLAUDE McKAY (1889–1948)

Claude McKay, whose poetry is said to have ushered in the Harlem Renaissance, was born to farmers in Clarendon Hills, Jamaica. Leaving at the age of six to study in Montego Bay, while living with his brother who was a teacher and a minister, McKay developed a distinctive poetic style and a passion for activism.

In 1912, at the age of twenty-five, McKay saw his first two volumes of poetry published. *Songs of Jamaica* and *Constab Ballads* were precursors to the protest poems that made McKay famous amongst the Renaissance artists. In the same year, he came to the United States to study agriculture at Tuskegee Institute under the esteemed George Washington Carver (see no. 29). He left the program within a year and took up agricultural studies at Kansas State College. He quit that program after two years and committed himself entirely to the act of writing poetry and fiction.

It was in 1919 that McKay's poetry came to stand for the sentiments of a whole new generation eager to fight continually for equality. "If We Must Die" punctuated the bloody summer of 1919:

*If we must die—let it not be like bogs*
*Hunted and penned in an inglorious spot, . . .*
*Though far outnumbered, let us show us brave,*
*And for their thousand blows deal one death-blow!*
*What though before us lies the open grave?*
*Like men we'll face the murderous, cowardly pack,*
*Pressed to the wall, dying, but fighting back!*

The volatile decade that followed brought an explosion of powerful literature, music, and visual arts. The wild life of Harlem, envied by many white Americans and written about by James Weldon Johnson (see no. 36) and Langston Hughes (see no. 64), also fed the artistic life of McKay.

In 1920, *Spring in New Hampshire*, his next volume, was published and soon followed by *Harlem Shadows* (1922). His first novel, *Home to Harlem*, was released in 1928, followed by *Banjo: A Story Without a Plot* (1929), and *Banana Bottom* (1933).

A great critic of Marcus Garvey's Back-to-Africa movement (see no. 46), McKay not only used his talent to inspire and entertain but to publicly oppose what he considered a threat to African Americans.

"The most puzzling thing about the 'Back-to-Africa' propaganda is the leader's repudiation of all the fundamentals of the black worker's economic struggle. . . . All those who think broadly on social conditions are amazed at Garvey's ignorance and his intolerance to modem social ideas."

McKay traveled extensively though Europe before returning in 1934 to become a U.S. citizen and to write his autobiography, *A Long Way From Home* (1940). In 1944, he converted to Roman Catholicism and worked among the poor in Chicago until his death in 1948.

**Claude McKay**

# 48. A. PHILIP RANDOLPH
(1889–1979)

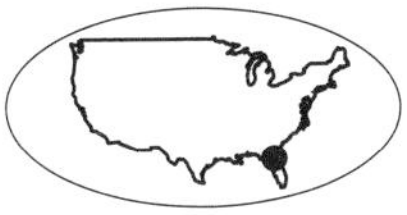

Asa Philip Randolph, one of the nation's most successful African American labor organizers, was born in Crescent City, Florida, where he worked for his father's tailor shop before completing high school at Cookman Institute. He enrolled at the City College of New York, and while there, he worked enough odd jobs to note the consistent ill treatment of African American workers.

With a prophetic drive, Randolph attempted to unionize shipyard workers during World War I, although he never succeeded. He co-founded the socialist paper *The Messenger* in 1917 before founding The Brotherhood of Sleeping Car Porters & Maids in 1925. As the first African American trade union, the Brotherhood took some twelve years to gain recognition from the Pullman Company.

**A. Philip Randolph**

Organizing labor unions put Randolph in opposition to one of the popular leaders of his day, Marcus Garvey (see no. 46) and his Back-to-Africa movement. Randolph said of him, "What you needed to follow Garvey was a leap of the imagination, but socialism and trade unionism called for rigorous social struggle." However, Garvey's popularity inspired Randolph. Co-founding the National Negro Congress in 1936 and serving as its first president, Randolph began to organize the mass demonstrations and parades that had been so effective for Garvey. He became such a popular public figure that his persuasive promise to schedule a 100,000 person march on Washington in 1941 convinced President Franklin Roosevelt to issue the first ban on racial discrimination within the military. Roosevelt's order allowed a measure of equality in the armed forces, including shared quarters and shared duties, and Randolph realized how powerful mass protest could be.

In 1963, as his crowning achievement, A. Philip Randolph brought 250,000 people to Washington, D.C., to demand freedom and equality in America. After years of segregation, low wages, and unequal rights, the crowd who'd come at Randolph's invitation was treated to speakers Dr. Martin Luther King Jr. (see no. 91), Roy Wilkins (see no. 62), John Lewis of the Student Nonviolent Coordinating Committee, and many other celebrities of the movement. His organizational skill led to a mass gathering of people ready to accept the message of the civil rights movement. Together, the nation strove for greater equality in the workforce and a greater awareness among all Americans. As Randolph once said, "By fighting for their rights now, American Negroes are helping to make America a moral and spiritual arsenal of democracy. Their fight against the poll tax, against lynch law, segregation, and Jim Crow, their fight for economic, political, and social equality, thus becomes part of the global war for freedom."

# 49. MORDECAI W. JOHNSON
(1890–1979)

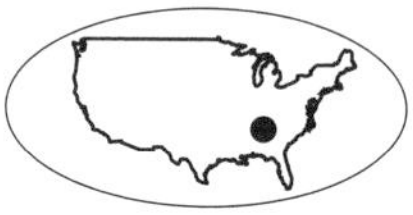

**Mordecai W. Johnson**

Mordecai W. Johnson, who as the president of Howard University pioneered programs of African American education, was born in Paris, Tennessee, into the family of a minister at the Mt. Zion Baptist Church. He studied religion extensively, earning a B.A. from Morehouse College by the age of sixteen, a B.A. from the University of Chicago, a bachelor of Divinity (B.D.) from Rochester Theological Seminary, a Master in Theology (M.Th.) from Harvard, and a Doctor of Divinity (D.D.) from both Howard University and Gammon Theological Seminary in 1928.

In 1926, Mordecai Johnson became the first African American president of Howard University. He succeeded a man who had fired Alain Locke because Locke had wanted to make Howard a school driven by African American culture. Johnson made it his goal to equip African American students for higher education. He rehired Locke and invited the most esteemed African American thinkers, including Charles Houston (see no. 55), Carter Woodson (see no. 43), and Benjamin Mays (see no. 56) to teach. He doubled the size of the university's libraries and added twenty new buildings to its campus.

"The Negro people haw been with us here for three hundred years. . . . Now they have come to the place where their faith can no longer feed on the bread of repression and violence. They ask for the bread of liberty, of public equality, and public responsibility. It must not he denied them."

Johnson's belief that the United States owed equal education, equal responsibility, and equal respect to African Americans was one that colored his entire thirty-year tenure at Howard. He believed in the teaching of critical analysis; he believed in the power of Christianity; and he believed, unlike Marcus Garvey (see no. 46) and his supporters, that democracy was to be found in the United States, if each American took his place in its defense.

Under Johnson's leadership, Howard grew into one of the nation's most successful educational institutions for African Americans. His goal was to prepare his students for equality and arm them with the skills of critical thinking and higher thought. Programs, such as Locke's envisioned African Studies, were given the freedom to grow and influence a nation's ideas of education. Finally, there was another well-funded, highly esteemed school on the level of the famed Tuskegee Institute, and many Howard graduates are now among the most influential NAACP and civil rights activists.

# 50. BESSIE COLEMAN (1892–1926)

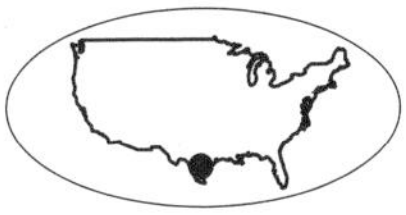

Bessie Coleman, the first African American female aviator, was born in Atlanta, Texas, where she grew up promising to make something of herself. The family entertainer, accountant, and intellect, Bessie completed her education in a one room schoolhouse that closed during every cotton-picking season. She worked as a laundress to earn enough money to move to Langston, Oklahoma, to attend the Colored Agricultural & Normal University. After one semester in remedial courses, her funds ran out. She returned to her mother in Waxahachie, Texas.

In 1915, Bessie moved to Chicago to live with her brother. Employed as a manicurist on Chicago's State Street, Bessie met all the notorious figures in crime, nightclubs, gambling, and alcohol. She watched them profit as Prohibition transformed Chicago into a city full of danger and illegal pleasures.

One day, one of her brothers aimed an insult at African American women that was meant particularly for Bessie. While talking about the French women pilots he'd served with, John Coleman said "You . . . women ain't never goin' to fly. Not like those women I saw in France." Without knowing it, he gave Bessie just the thing she needed to hear. "That's it," she responded. "You just called it for me."

Unable to train for a license anywhere in the United States, Bessie went to her friend Robert Abbott (see no. 35), publisher of *The Chicago Defender*, and enlisted his help, among others, to secure passage to Europe and tuition to the finest school in France, Ecole d'Aviation des Freres Caudron.

Bessie returned to the United States a celebrity in 1921. Determined to attract other African Americans to aviation, she began lecturing at schools and churches, and started giving demonstrations of extreme skill, sometimes pulling a plane out of a nosedive mere feet from the ground. She was daring,

**Bessie Coleman**

dramatic, and considered one of the most beautiful women of the age.

Bessie was always trying to excel. Deciding to open up an aviation school, she saved up for a plane and traveled around, offering flights, performing feats, and giving lectures until she could purchase it.

On April 30, she flew with a novice pilot who was helping her scout out the airfield she would parachute into at the Jacksonville Negro Welfare League's annual Field Day. Bessie didn't bother to buckle her seat belt, as she would have to lean out of the little Curtiss JN4 to see where she wanted to plan her landing for the next day.

Surprisingly, with pilot William Wills at the controls, the plane sped from 80 to 110 miles per hour, fell into a nosedive, then went into a tailspin at 1,000 feet, flipping at 500 feet, and dropping Bessie Coleman to her death. The cause was later found to be a wrench that had lodged in the control gears.

Rediscovered by contemporary aviators, Coleman is now considered an aviation pioneer, and each year, on the anniversary of her death, historian Rufus A. Hunt flies over her grave, dropping flowers from his plane. In addition, the U.S. Post Office has finally honored Coleman and her achievements with a stamp.

# 51. FREDERICK McKINLEY JONES (1893–1961)

**Frederick McKinley Jones**

Frederick McKinley Jones's inventions revolutionized the refrigeration units used on trucks, trains, and airplanes so that foods and medicines could be transported safely all over the world. He was born in Cincinnati, Ohio, where he was orphaned when he was nine years old. Sent to live with a priest in Kentucky, Jones was schooled in the Catholic faith until he left for Hallock, Minnesota, in 1912. He worked fixing farm equipment while studying mechanical engineering. Returning to Minnesota after serving in World War I, Jones became interested in race cars and the entertainment industry. He built Hallock's first radio station transmitter and a soundtrack system for motion pictures.

Fascinated with the challenges of machines, Jones was very interested when he overheard his boss, Joseph A. Numero, puzzling over the problem of refrigeration in trucks that had to transport temperature-sensitive cargo. There were refrigerating devices at the time, but they were unable to withstand the movement of the trucks, and they took up valuable space.

With these concerns in mind, Jones began to experiment with new refrigerator designs. First he attached a unit to the bottom of the truck, learning quickly that mud would inevitably clog it up and destroy it. When he attached a unit to the top of a truck, Jones knew he'd found the answer.

Not only did Jones recognize the numerous possibilities, but his boss did as well. Forming the U.S. Thermo Control Company, Jones and Numero began to refrigerate not only trucks, but planes, ships, and trains.

Receiving more than sixty patents for his inventions—forty for refrigeration alone—Jones made it possible for the nation, and then the world, to transport fresh fruits, vegetables, dairy products and meat to any destination through refrigerated storage. His shock-resistant refrigeration units led to a new frozen food industry in America.

Although Jones's inventions were originally used for commercial transportation, it soon became apparent that medicinal transportation could be lifesaving. During World War II, it was Jones's original designs that made it possible for blood and medicine to be kept fresh for the victims of warfare. Jones was a creative genius and a lifesaver of American soldiers.

# 52. WALTER F. WHITE
(1893–1955)

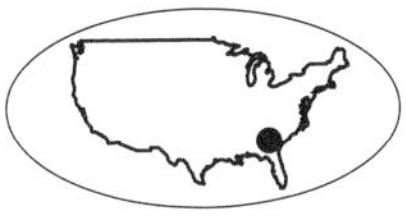

Walter White, who served a highly influential term as executive secretary for the National Association for the Advancement of Colored People (NAACP), was born in Atlanta, Georgia. He attended segregated schools before entering Atlanta University and graduating in 1916. He joined a local branch of the NAACP and served as local secretary, carrying off management affairs with such dependable skill that James Weldon Johnson (see no. 36) befriended him, recommending him for assistant secretary of the New York office.

White took great interest in the anti-lynching campaign headed by Ida B. Wells-Barnett (see no. 27) and became one of the spokesmen who effectively reported on violent crime against African Americans. Using his light complexion to help him pass as a white journalist, he was able to infiltrate lynching areas safely and bring out the stories that were hardest to obtain.

Along with his steady, influential voice in the NAACP, White possessed a voice of great creative strength. He joined the other writers and artists of the Harlem Renaissance with three books published between 1920 and 1926: *Rope and Faggot* (1920), *The Fire in the Flint* (1924) and *Flight* (1926).

A powerful manager and tireless activist, White, as executive secretary of the NAACP, saw the association's work begin to turn the tides of racism. He supported sharecroppers and tenant farmers in their efforts to organize, and he watched the U.S. Supreme Court rule in favor of the founding of the Progressive Farmers Household Union of America. The ruling, passed on Moore v. Dempsey, allowed farmers to move out from under the servitude enforced by the sharecropping "accounting" system that kept them poor by design. White also supported A. Philip Randolph (see no. 48) when Randolph met with President Franklin D. Roosevelt and promised that if all military personnel weren't desegregated quickly, 100,000 people would accept his impassioned invitation to march on Washington. White was also influential in removing W. E. B. Du Bois (sec no. 32) from his position as editor of *Crisis* and director of research and publicity. Du Bois was removed because his support for voluntary segregation violated the stated goal of the NAACP: "The Negro must, without yielding, continue the grim struggle for integration and against segregation for his own physical, moral and spiritual well-being and for that of white America and of the world at large."

**Walter F. White**

# 53. E. FRANKLIN FRAZIER (1894–1962)

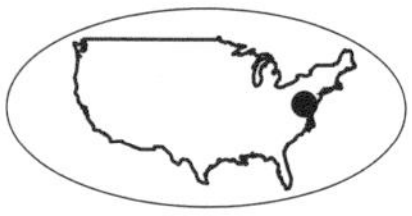

**E. Franklin Frazier**

E. Franklin Frazier, the great sociologist and educator, was born in Baltimore, Maryland. He graduated from Howard University in 1916 and taught at numerous schools before returning to his own education at Clark University in Massachusetts. His real passion was sociology, the behaviors of different racial groups, which he studied at Clark and at the University of Chicago, where he earned a Ph.D. in 1931.

Beginning a career as an educator and sociologist, Frazier taught first at Morehouse College before being invited to direct Atlanta University's School of Social Work in 1922. He then taught at Fisk University from 1931 to 1934, before accepting the post as head of Howard University's Department of Sociology, which he kept until 1959.

Author Columbus Salley has said of E. Franklin Frazier that he was "to black sociology what Carter Woodson (see no. 43) became to black history: the father and leading pioneer." Studying the African-American experience sociologically, Frazier was able to discover patterns of behavior and to identify their positive uses: "A few choice souls may rise to a moral elevation where they can love those who oppress them. But the mass of mankind either become accommodated to an enforced inferior status with sentiments consonant with their situation, or save themselves by hating the oppression and the oppressors. In the latter case, hatred is a positive moral force."

By trying to understand the black response to a society dominated by a majority of another race, Frazier could then speak to both about how to better understand one another.

To this end, Frazier published many books and essays that dissected the sociological reality of race relations. *Traditions and Patterns of Negro Family Life* was published in 1934, *The Negro Family in the United States* in 1939, *The Negro in the United States* in 1949, *Race and Culture Contacts in the Modern World* and the controversial *Black Bourgeoisie* in 1957, and the *Negro Church in America* in 1962, the year of his death.

Frazier, as one of the brightest men studying racial tension, was able to take the fear away from conflict and the shame away from African Americans living in an often hostile environment. Frazier destigmatized African American anger and made it possible to look to the racist as well as the victim, in order to understand the cause and effect of race relations.

# 54. BESSIE SMITH (1894–1937)

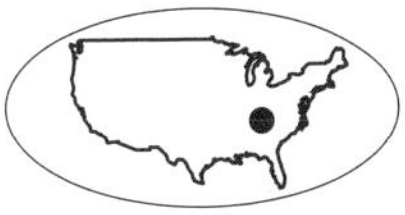

Bessie Smith, "Empress of the Blues," was born in Chattanooga, Tennessee, where she grew up with her six siblings. Her parents died at a very young age, so Bessie grew up under the care of her older sister Viola.

Bessie grew up in harsh poverty, but she had music, and all the emotional power of a world-class performer. Retreating early into the solace of blues rhythms, Bessie started singing with her young voice on the streets for nickels and dimes when she was only nine years old.

When she was eighteen, Bessie obtained her first part in a show. One of her first big fans was the famous blues singer Gertrude "Ma" Rainey. Having launched a lifetime career, Smith began to travel throughout the South, singing everywhere. She could be found in clubs, theaters, anywhere people could gather.

Traveling in the South meant living daily with segregation and the threat inherent in being a new African American woman in racist towns where she wasn't protected by her reputation as a singer. A safe place to sleep was hard to come by, as was a desegregated restaurant, or a seat on the bus.

As George Hoefer wrote, "Her blues could be funny and boisterous and gentle and angry and bleak, but underneath all of them ran the raw bitterness of being a human being who had to think twice about which toilet she could use. You cannot hear Bessie without hearing why Dr. Martin Luther King Jr. doesn't want to wait anymore."

Even though Smith dealt with a lot of racism, she was not often afraid. Once threatened by a group of Ku Klux Klan members, Bessie chased them out, crying, "You better pick up them sheets and run!"

She was a big, powerful woman who by 1920 had grown into one of the nation's favorite blues singers. Crossing all race lines, Bessie drew massive crowds with her voice and attracted some of the best musicians, including Charlie Green, Louis Armstrong (see no. 60), and Benny Goodman, who were honored to back her up.

She made her first record in 1923, called it "Down Hearted Blues" and watched it sell more than two million copies during a year in which Columbia Studios had even considered going out of business. Bessie herself lived like a queen, making enough money that she could be effusively generous, which hurt her later, when the Depression hit in 1929.

Bessie went back on the road, back to the harsh conditions of traveling, although poverty cut back the number of people who could afford to see her or buy her brilliant recordings. While on the road, she was critically injured in a car crash and taken to a Negro Hospital in Clarksdale, Mississippi, where she died.

**Bessie Smith**

# 55. CHARLES H. HOUSTON (1895–1950)

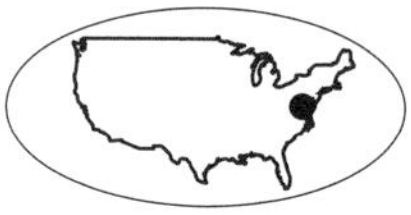

Charles H. Houston, an influential civil rights lawyer and the designer of Howard University's Law School—which came to lead the world in the training of African American lawyers—was born the grandson of an Underground Railroad "engineer" in Washington, D.C. He attended the nation's first black high school, M Street High, and went on to Amherst College at the age of fifteen, where he was elected to Phi Beta Kappa.

By 1915, he was teaching English at Howard University, which he did for two years before entering into the service during World War I. He was made a second lieutenant field artillery officer, but he was still subjected to life-threatening racism. Upon his return, Houston entered Harvard Law School.

After editing the *Harvard Law Review*, receiving a Ph.D. from Harvard, and doing post-doctoral work in Madrid, he was accepted into the Washington, D.C., bar in 1924. He was then invited to teach at Howard University, which was already turning out 25 percent of the nation's African American lawyers.

In 1929, Houston launched a massive program destined to turn Howard Law School into the world's finest school for African American lawyers, "the West Point of Negro leadership." Promoting the idea that a new approach to law would help African American lawyers influence government policy, economic freedom, and social systems, Houston not only redesigned Howard's policy, but the nation's. Building a place where young lawyers like Thurgood Marshall (see no. 67) could be trained as "civil engineers," Houston began a second program to slowly chip away at the roots of the Jim Crow system, the set of laws that made segregation and racism legal and very difficult to rise above.

The first case was against the University of North Carolina in 1933. It was lost on a technicality. The second was fought by Marshall, who convinced the Maryland Court of Appeals to force the University of Maryland to admit Donald Murray. Case by case, Houston and his associates attacked Jim Crow laws, until they broke through.

It was Houston's tireless work that kept the "separate but equal" doctrine of Plessy v. Fergusson from succeeding in all cases. The final battle, Brown v. Board of Education, was fought by Thurgood Marshall, who had followed Houston passionately. Without him, the U.S. Supreme Court may not have declared segregation of public schools illegal in 1954, four years after Houston's death.

In 1934, Houston was asked to direct both the Joint Committee of the NAACP and the American Fund for Public Service, both of which drove passionately toward desegregation.

Houston's influence on men like Thurgood Marshall was invaluable to the fight for equality, and his influence on Howard University made it possible for African Americans to educate themselves in the word of law and defend themselves in United States courts.

**Charles H. Houston**

# 56. BENJAMIN E. MAYS (1895–1984)

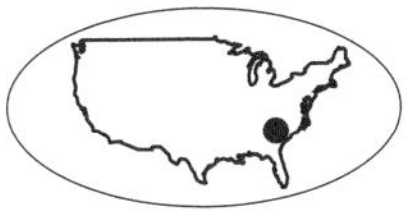

**Benjamin E. Mays**

Benjamin E. Mays taught many young men, including Dr. Martin Luther King Jr. (see no. 91), how to turn their finest ideals into a reality. He is one of the men who live on as an example and an educator.

Born to former slaves in Epworth, South Carolina, Mays experienced the violence between races firsthand when his father was attacked by a mob in what is known as the Phoenix Riot of 1898. Mays was only four years old at the time.

Mays was educated in a segregated school, from which he graduated valedictorian before attending Bates College in Maine, where he was elected Phi Beta Kappa.

Mays decided early after graduation to enter the ministry. He worked for his M.A. and Ph.D. from the University of Chicago, and he served as pastor of the Shiloh Baptist Church in Atlanta, Georgia. Dedicated to integration and desegregation in the United States, Mays melded a bond between academia and the church that helped African Americans work together to fight policies such as the "separate but equal" doctrine put forth in the case of Plessy v. Fergusson. He said, "We strive to desegregate and integrate America to the end that this great nation of ours . . . will truly become the lighthouse of freedom where none will be denied because his skin is black and none favored because his eyes are blue."

To educate all African Americans on the value of the church in their struggle, Mays and Joseph W. Nicholson wrote *The Negro's Church* in 1930. (Mays continued his discourse in *The Negro's God*, published in 1968.)

In 1934, Mordecai Johnson (see no. 49) invited Mays to join Howard University as the dean of the School of Religion. Here, working with students like Dr. Martin Luther King Jr., Mays's influence was invaluable in teaching modern leaders that the church could accompany them as a tool for the ideal of equality. His stirring sermons and brilliant lectures gave him a position as one of the most influential religious activists in the United States.

In 1940, Mays left Howard to become president of Morehouse College, an institution known for the quality of its graduates in the fields of medicine, law, engineering, and religion. He stayed until 1967, when he was elected to the Atlanta School Board, over which he presided until his retirement in 1981.

# 57. PAUL ROBESON
(1898–1976)

**Paul Robeson**

Paul Robeson, the man of a million talents who applied himself to athletics, acting, and civil rights leadership, was the son of a man who had escaped slavery and a woman who died when Paul was still a young boy. Born in Princeton, New Jersey, and educated primarily in Somerville, Robeson showed an early and exceptional intellect. He was elected into the Phi Beta Kappa fraternity in his junior year at Rutgers University and earned twelve letters in various sports, including football. He was named All-American twice—the first African American to win that honor. He graduated as the class valedictorian in 1919 and played professional football to work his way through Columbia University Law School. Completing his degree in two years, Robeson emerged from Columbia twenty-five years old and already turning his passion to a new career—acting.

Eugene O'Neill, one of the world's respected playwrights, saw Robeson perform and offered him the lead in his great play *All God's Chillun Got Wings* (1925). Next, Robeson was offered a role in O'Neill's famous *Emperor Jones*. Finding a new interest in music that matched his love for sports, learning, and theater, Robeson accepted composer Jerome Kern's offer to play Joe in *Showboat*. With his booming, rich voice, Robeson made the song "Ol' Man River" a national favorite.

Traveling abroad, Robeson built faithful audiences all over Europe, and in 1931, he accepted the role of a lifetime: "There has never been and never will be a finer rendition of this particular tragedy. It is unbelievably magnificent." This was the sentiment repeated over and over again in the reviews for Robeson's never-to-be-equaled performance of Shakespeare's *Othello*.

Mastering everything he attempted, Robeson moved on quickly. Taking up an interest in politics and race, Robeson became one of the best educated and eloquent speakers of the early twentieth century. Learning more than twenty languages so that he might understand the cultures of twenty different peoples, Robeson studied different political systems, claiming publicly that the Soviet Union was a better friend to African peoples than the United States. He co-founded the Council of African Affairs in 1937, embracing socialism because it included racial equality. He marched on Washington, protested lynching, and refused to perform for segregated audiences.

His opinions, no matter how egalitarian, brought him to the end of his career. His defense of the Soviet Union during the red scare led the U.S. State Department to pull his passport. Unable to tour abroad and blacklisted by the entertainment industry for his socialist ideas, Robeson was unable to work. No one in the industry would hire him.

Robeson moved back to Harlem, New York, and settled in. In 1958, his passport was returned. Though he tried to return to his singing career, illness forbade it, and Robeson lived quietly in Harlem and Philadelphia until his death.

# 58. DUKE ELLINGTON (1899–1974)

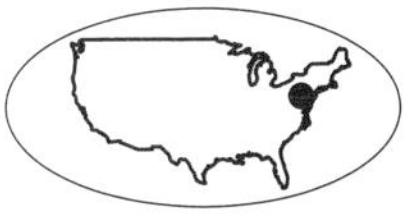

Edward Kennedy Ellington, called Duke by fellow musicians because of his style and manners, was born in Washington, D.C., where he was educated in segregated schools. He dropped out of high school as a senior and took up music professionally, although he was offered a scholarship to Pratt Institute in New York City for his skill as an artist. Writing his first song at seventeen, "The Soda Fountain Rag," about the Poodle Dog Cafe where he worked after school, Ellington formed a band called The Washingtonians and took it to New York City in 1922.

**Duke Ellington**

Though the first trip did little more than introduce the band to influential musicians like Fats Waller and Willy Smith, their second trip in 1923 landed a gig at the Hollywood Club. They settled in, and within four years the Washingtonians were playing the legendary Cotton Club. After five years on stage and on radio shows recorded at the Cotton Club, Ellington had gained a wide reputation as one of the finest composers in the United States. His "East St. Louis Toodle-Oo," "Mood Indigo," and "The Mooche" all became big hits and crossed over to a European audience.

Touring Europe and writing innovative pieces such as "Black, Brown and Beige," "Sophisticated Lady," and "The A Train," Ellington weathered the Depression and World War II, appeared in films, and used the "African pulse" to create compositions that gained him respect throughout his life.

"The common root, of course, comes out of Africa. That's the pulse. The African Pulse. Its all the way back from what they first recognized as the old slave chants and up through the blues, the jazz, and up through the rock. And the avant garde. And it's all got the African pulse."

Even Ellington's voice had a rhythm and a pulse. As the musical ambassador for the U.S. State Department, Ellington toured the Middle and Far East in the 1960s, using style and world-class rhythm to ignite respect. Prolific until his death in 1974, he conducted his own *Golden Broom* and the Golden Apple in 1965 at Lincoln Center, conducted at Grace Cathedral in San Francisco in 1965, and was elected to the elite National Institute of Arts & Letters in 1970.

His musical portfolio includes more than nine hundred compositions, among them some of America's most exquisite. He was a welcome performer everywhere and enchanted audiences everywhere.

## 59. PERCY LAVON JULIAN (1899–1975)

**Percy Lavon Julian**

Percy Lavon Julian, the creator of a drug that saved thousands from developing blindness, was born in Montgomery, Alabama, where his education was so poor that he had to enter remedial courses to meet his first year requirements at DePauw University. Determined and intelligent, Julian improved immensely, graduating as the valedictorian of his class.

Though Julian's record was excellent and his determination to study chemistry exceptional, top-rated graduate schools were still lumbering under segregationist policies. Julian taught chemistry at Fisk University for two years before Harvard accepted him as a student. After completing his graduate degree, Julian went back to teaching, working first at West Virginia State College and later at Howard University in Washington, D.C. His doctorate was completed in Vienna, where Julian first started to experiment with the medicinal properties of soybeans.

Returning to the United States, Julian used his results to create a new drug that fought the effects of glaucoma, a debilitating disease that resulted in blindness. Physostigmine was such a breakthrough that Dean Blanchard from DePauw University quickly recommended that Julian be invited to head the university's chemistry department. Though he'd graduated valedictorian and gone on to produce an invaluable drug, racial prejudice again kept him from being offered the position.

One person who was not concerned with Julian's race was W. J. O'Brien of the Glidden Paint Company. Hiring Julian to work as Glidden's head chemist, O'Brien's foresight turned a company suffering from heavy losses into a prosperous one.

Julian opened his own pharmaceutical company in 1953. Julian Laboratories became an overnight success, but its creator continued researching and working toward the relief of pain and the extension of life, accepting numerous awards and an honorary Ph.D. from DePauw University.

During his life, Julian developed more than one hundred patents, including Aero-Foam, used as an extinguisher of gas and oil fires during World War II; a hormone made from soy beans that treated some forms of cancer; and a system for manufacturing cortisone that was used against arthritis. Working always toward the greater health of all people, he produced numerous lifesaving products that furthered the evolution of medicine.

# 60. LOUIS ARMSTRONG
(1900–1971)

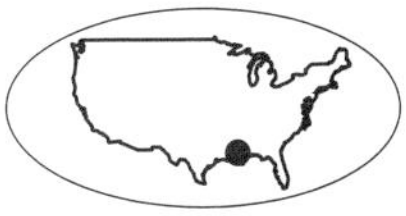

Daniel Louis Armstrong, the innovative trumpet player known for revolutionizing jazz, was born in New Orleans, where his parents divorced when he was five. Living in a ghetto of the city where he was poorly educated, Armstrong was thrown into the Waif's Home for Boys when he fired a pistol into the air on New Year's Eve. He was twelve years old, and this unfortunate circumstance was the event that turned his life around.

While in the boys' home, Armstrong met Peter Davis, a cornet player who taught Louis how to play his first instrument. By the time he was released at age fifteen, Armstrong was a fine enough cornet player to become a student of Joe "King" Oliver. Oliver was a popular jazz cornetist who not only taught Armstrong the trumpet, for which he would become famous, but procured him occasional gigs with Kid Ory's Band. Until 1919, Armstrong played as Oliver's backup, even taking his place when Oliver was out of town on tour. In 1922, Oliver and Armstrong paired up again in Chicago, this time playing on stage side by side. By 1924, when Armstrong took a job with the Fletcher Henderson Band in New York, jazz enthusiasts were already saying that Armstrong was the better player. By the time he returned to Chicago and organized his own band, the "Hot Five," word had spread that he was the best in the United States.

The "Hot Five" grew into the "Hot Seven," and songs like "Heebie Jeebies" and "West End Blues" became hits favored in the United States and abroad. After starring in the musical *Hot Chocolates* in New York, he traveled to Europe, playing for King George VI and a crowd of more than 100,000 in Ghana in 1960.

Affectionately nicknamed "Satchel-mouth," and later "Satchmo," while performing at the London Palladium in 1932, Armstrong gained a notoriety, respect, and familiarity amongst his fans, both for his personality and his musical definition of the black American soul.

**Lois Armstrong**

Respected as a masterful soloist, known internationally for his manner, and nicknamed "The Ambassador of Good Will" for his effect on audiences, Armstrong continued to expand musically. His experiments brought new respect to the culture that had given the world its most soulful and celebratory sounds. Hugues Panassie, a noted expert on jazz, said of him, "The whole of jazz music was transformed by Louis, overthrown by his genius. In Louis Armstrong's music is the New Orleans style at its peak, and also the basis of almost all styles that were derived from it, directly or indirectly."

Armstrong's creative style surpassed even his instrument. Traveling throughout the world, Armstrong kept evolving, producing a new form of singing called "scat," in which simple syllables and their rhythms become the lyrics, making the voice an instrument of music that communicates through sounds instead of words.

# 61. ZORA NEALE HURSTON
(1901–1960)

**Zora Neale Hurston**

Zora Neale Hurston, one of the celebrated writers of the Harlem Renaissance, grew up in a family of eight children in Eatonville, Florida. She lost her mother when she was nine and was raised by her father, who later became the mayor of Eatonville. Determined to follow her mother's advise and jump at the Sun, Hurston left home as a teenager and was self-supporting by the age of fourteen.

Working as a costumer and a maid for a Gilbert and Sullivan traveling show, Hurston moved to Baltimore, where she attended Morgan Academy, graduating in 1918. Following her passion to Howard University, Hurston found the mentors that could fuel her interest in the folklore and history of African Americans. Alain Locke took a great interest in her work and helped her develop the style that would become famous in her short stories, novels, and works of folklore.

Hurston's short story "John Redding Goes to Sea" was picked up by *Stylus* in 1921, and three years later her second story, "Drenched in Light," was published in the National Urban League's *Opportunity.*

Her work was well-received, and in 1925, Hurston accepted a scholarship to attend Bamard College in New York, where she studied anthropology. While there, Langston Hughes (see no. 64), another brilliant writer of the Renaissance, collaborated with her on a magazine called *Fire!*, designed to, as Hughes said, "bum up a lot of the old, dead, conventional Negro-white ideas of the past." Unfortunately, and ironically, their entire inventory was destroyed by fire. They teamed up again in 1930 to write the play *Mule Bone.*

Though Hurston came under the same criticism as Paul Laurence Dunbar (see no. 37) for presenting stereotypical images, her work has more recently been seen as a creative body detailing the struggle of a people in transition. She was a great observer, a woman who could translate for a broad twentieth-century audience, black and white, the folk history that created black America.

Among Hurston's important works are the short story "Spunk" (1925), published in Alain Locke's *The New Negro*, and her folk-loric pieces, including *Jonah's Gourd Vine* (1934), *Mules and Men* (1935), *Tell My Horse* (1938), *Man of the Mountain* (1939), her very popular novel *Their Eyes Were Watching God* (1937), and her autobiographical work, *Dust Tracks on the Road* (1942).

She lost much of her audience in the 1940s, as protest literature became more popular. She was falsely accused of sexually molesting a child, and retreated, taking jobs as a maid, a librarian, and a substitute teacher.

Hurston died in poverty, but there was little tragedy in her life. As stated by biographer Robert E. Hemenway, "She personally believed in an integrated society, but she spent her career trying to preserve and celebrate black cultural practices."

# 62. ROY WILKINS (1901–1981)

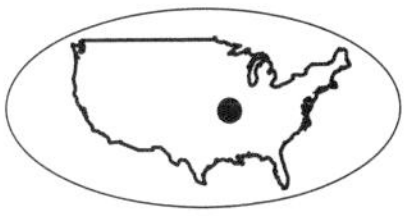

Roy Willdns was executive secretary for the NAACP from 1949 to 1977, making him the leader of one of the most powerful African American associations through the turbulent years of the civil rights movement. He was born in St. Louis, Missouri, but was raised by his aunt and uncle in St. Paul, Minnesota after his mother died of tuberculosis. Graduating from the University of Minnesota, where he'd edited the school newspaper and the *St. Paul Appeal*, Wilkins took a job on the *Kansas City Call*. He volunteered with the NAACP throughout his college career, but it wasn't until 1931 that Wilkins left the *Call* to join the NAACP as assistant executive secretary under Walter White.

In agreement with the established agenda of the NAACP, Wilkins supported desegregation on all levels. He was a writer who reported on the violence so prevalent against African Americans, and he succeeded W. E. B. Du Bois (see no. 32) as editor of *Crisis* in 1934.

In 1949, when White took a leave of absence, Wilkins stepped in as acting secretary, and even after White's return, he retained the authority to accomplish many of the daily duties of the job. In 1955, after White's death, Wilkins took up the role of executive secretary again, this time keeping the post for two decades and moving the NAACP through its delicate transition from leading civil rights organization to its new position as one among many organizations, including the militant Black Panthers and the Student Nonviolent Coordinating Committee. When young people were being arrested for sit-ins that peacefully protested the segregation of public lunch counters, Wilkins not only requested that the NAACP post bail, he submitted himself to arrest. In his own words, "We have always used persuasion through various means of political and economic pressure, but now we're going to use it much more intensely than in the past because the membership has become restless over the slow pace of the civil rights proceedings."

Wilkins was one of the chief organizers of the massive March on Washington in 1963. Helping A. Philip Randolph (see no. 48) bring 225,000 people out to hear Dr. Martin Luther King Jr. (see no. 91) speak in support of civil rights, Wilkins waged one of the most successful protests in American history. He put the association's support behind the Civil Rights Act of 1964 and chaired the momentous Leadership Conference on Civil Rights.

After riots broke out into the Watts district of Los Angeles in 1965, Wilkins was one of the members of the Kemer Commission, organized to analyze the social causes. They brought this statement to the fore of the American mind: "Our nation is moving toward two societies, one black, one white—separate and unequal." Attacking the social roots of unequal societies, Wilkins and the NAACP supported the passage of the 1965 Voting Rights Act and the 1968 Fair Housing Act.

Wilkins retired from the NAACP in 1977, succeeded by executive secretary Benjamin Hooks, who followed him in the fight for equality in America.

**Roy Wilkins**

# 63. MARIAN ANDERSON
(1902–1993)

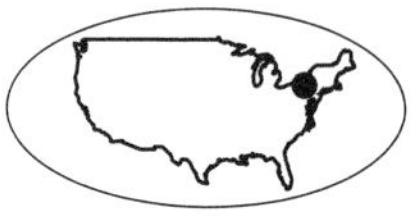

**Marian Anderson**

Marian Anderson, "the best opera singer in the world," was born in Philadelphia, Pennsylvania, where she picked up an interest in singing from her parents, who both sang in church. Marian joined the junior chorus at the Union Baptist Church, studied under her father, and was acknowledged as an upcoming star by the age of eight.

After singing her way through elementary school, Anderson joined the Philadelphia Choral Society in high school. When she was a senior, her church congregation sponsored her professional training with world-renowned voice teacher Giuseppe Boghetti. They worked together continually as student and mentor until Boghetti's death.

After being refused by an all-white voice school, Anderson went professional. She performed at the Town Hall in New York City when she was twenty but learned one of her most valuable lessons when she entered the performance ill-prepared and sang so poorly that she considered quitting. After suffering this disappointment, she decided to work even harder, entering a competition in 1925 and winning the Lewisohn Stadium Concert Award. Her career had officially begun.

Anderson soloed with the New York Philharmonic Orchestra. She toured nationally and then internationally. In South America, Asia, and the United States, Marian Anderson played exclusively to sold out houses. Her critics began to publish statements such as, "what I heard today one is privileged to hear only in a hundred years." She had readied a pinnacle of international appeal, but one event in 1939 made her more than a brilliant contralto, it made her a symbol of African American pride.

Though Anderson had studied with the world's greats and even played Carnegie Hall, when Howard University sought to bring her to Constitution Hall in Washington, D.C., the Daughters of the American Revolution (DAR) rejected the request based on Marian Andersen' s race.

The protest was deafening. First Lady Eleanor Roosevelt resigned from the DAR. Eloquent letters, both proud and outraged, hit papers all over the nation. The Secretary of the Interior, Harold Ickes, with the help of Eleanor Roosevelt, scheduled a new appearance at the Lincoln Memorial, and 75,000 people came to hear the world's best living singer perform "The Star-Spangled Banner," "America," and "My Soul is Anchored in the Lord." Marian Anderson found herself a symbol for more than excellence. She was proof that African Americans could unite as a powerful coalition and white Americans were willing to join them in the fight for equality.

Anderson retired in 1965, after accepting awards from the King of Sweden and the Emperor of Japan and after becoming the first African American member of the Metropolitan Opera. She also sang at the inaugurations of Dwight D. Eisenhower and John F. Kennedy.

# 64. LANGSTON HUGHES (1902–1967)

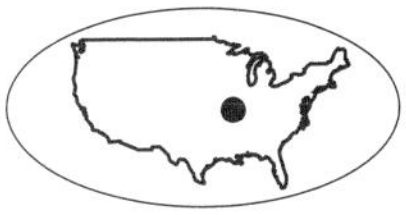

Langston Hughes, called "the Poet Laureate of the Negro Race," was born in Joplin, Missouri, but raised in different cities around the Midwest and in Mexico City. He graduated high school in 1920, and in 1921 the NAACP's *Crisis* launched his career by publishing "The Negro Speaks of Rivers," one of Hughes' first poems: "I've known rivers:/I've known rivers ancient as the world and older than the flow of human blood in human veins./My soul has grown deep like rivers. . . ."

Hughes became not only one of the first young poets to receive such honor from the NAACP, he was one of the first to signal the beginning of the Harlem Renaissance. One of the nation's most intense art movements, the Harlem Renaissance saw the rise of great writers like Hughes and Zora Neale Hurston (see no. 61), who later collaborated on both the publication *Fire!* and the play *Mule Bone*.

Hughes attended Columbia University for a year, but he was swept up by the music and excitement of Harlem and quit. After reveling in the art and music, he left the country to travel as a sailor, writing constantly. After returning to the United States, he published his first collection, *The Weary Blues*, in 1926. Hughes's poems were immediately well received. He went back to school at Lincoln University and published his second collection, *Fine Clothes to the Jew*, in 1927. Graduating in 1929, Hughes finished his novel *Not Without Laughter*, which was published in 1930.

Traveling constantly and writing constantly, Hughes began to publish in all genres. In 1934, after spending a year in Russia, his short stories were released in the collection *The Ways of White Folks*. He covered the Spanish Civil War as a correspondent, established the Harlem Suitcase Theatre, and produced his own play *Don't You Want to Be Free?*

Beginning a popular series for *The Chicago Defender* in 1934, Hughes created the character Jesse B. Semple, or "Simple," who appeared in five collections, beginning with *Simple Speaks His Mind* (1950) and ending with *Simple's Uncle Sam* (1965). A year after he began writing for the *Defender*, his play *Mulatto* opened a year-long run on Broadway.

Though Hughes retains his reputation as one of the most versatile and prolific of America's writers, he is remembered primarily as a poet. *Montage of a Dream Deferred* (1951), *Selected Poems* (1963) and *Panther and the Lash* (1967) remain some of the century's finest works.

Hughes worked consistently until his death, and his works gave new respect to the African American working class. Speaking of them in his essay "The Negro Artist and the Racial Mountain," he said: ". . . [J]azz is their child. They furnish a wealth of colorful, distinctive material for any artist because they still hold their own individuality in the face of American standardization."

**Langston Hughes**

# 65. RALPH BUNCHE (1904–1971)

**Ralph Bunche**

Ralph Bunche, who won the 1950 Nobel Peace Prize for his mediation during the Arab-Israeli conflict, was born in Detroit, Michigan. He moved to his grandmother's in Los Angeles, California, after losing his parents at the age of twelve.

Bunche graduated from Jefferson High School in 1922 and graduated summa cum laude and Phi Betta Kappa from the University of California in 1927. With a B.A. in international relations, he entered Harvard University and graduated with an M.A. in government in 1928. Taking an immediate position in the political science department of Howard University, Bunche assisted president Mordecai Johnson (see no. 49) for a year before beginning doctoral studies at Harvard.

Continuing with postdoctoral work in the United States and Britain after winning the Toppan Prize in 1934 for his dissertation, Bunche came to the attention of the Office of Strategic Services (OSS). During World War II, Bunche was hired by the OSS to assist the Joint Chiefs of Staff. He was then chosen to participate in the early planning sessions of the important new world council, the United Nations (UN). Bunche was made the director of the Trusteeship Division and was invited to serve on the special committee on Palestine.

After World War II, there was a great deal of highly sensitive mediation involved in partitioning Palestine in order to design the current state of Israel. In 1948, Ralph Bunche became the UN mediator in Palestine and designed the plan to divide Palestine into Jewish and Arab lands and place the coveted city of Jerusalem under UN supervision. The conflict between the Arabs and Israelis was a delicate situation and an important one to a world not yet recovered from World War II. In 1949, Bunche was able to bring about a truce, and in 1950, he was awarded the Nobel Peace Prize for bringing the conflict to a close. A highly respected mediator and a dedicated civil rights activist, Bunche used his influential name to support the NAACP and other civil rights leaders in the United States and Africa. He also continued to influence international politics through his appointment as the UN Undersecretary for Special Political Affairs. He was instrumental in the proceedings that brought an almost unanimous vote from the General Assembly to denounce apartheid and call for the release of political prisoners in South Africa.

Ralph Bunche resigned from the UN in 1971, after having used his entire career to support the ideals of peace and justice. He died without seeing the country of South Africa dismantle its system of apartheid, which was partly due to the American economic boycott.

# 66. DR. CHARLES R. DREW

(1904–1950)

Charles Drew, who revolutionized blood plasma research and developed the first blood banks, was born in Washington, D.C., where he grew up the oldest of five children. Graduating from M Street High School (now Paul Laurence Dunbar High School) with honors in 1922, Drew entered Amherst College, where he became an All-American football player. Even as he developed as an athlete, he maintained that his real interest was in medicine. Following graduation, Drew took a teaching position with Morgan College. He focused on teaching biology and leading the school's basketball and football teams to the championships until he was accepted at McGill University Medical School in Montreal, Canada. Fascinated with the challenges of blood research—the difficulty of keeping blood fresh and the problem of keeping all four blood types continually available—Drew began to experiment with plasma. He found that the blood's cells could be extracted, leaving the liquid intact. This liquid, or plasma, could be used in transfusions for all blood types and kept fresh for much longer than a week, which was the average for whole blood.

Drew's research, beginning at McGill and continuing through the 1930s at Howard University, became the basis of the blood work that saved thousands of lives during World War II.

In 1938, Drew left Howard on a leave, accepting a Rockefeller Foundation Grant in study at Columbia. As a resident in surgery at Columbia's Presbyterian Hospital. Drew took up his second field of interest, the preservation and storage of blood plasma. His excellent timing made it possible for the ideas in his doctoral thesis to revolutionize treatment of not just civilians in need of transfusions, but thousands of soldiers in the early 1940s.

Drew had returned to Howard in 1940, but he left again when the British Red Cross invited him to treat British soldiers through the Blood Transfusion Association's plasma processing program. In 1941, he returned to the United States and became director of the Red Cross Blood Bank in New York City, where he worked to supply plasma to U.S. soldiers.

In a famous conflict, the American Red Cross demanded that Drew not send "colored blood" to white troops overseas. If it was to be sent at all, it must be segregated. Confronting the medical ignorance of his associates, Drew announced: "Only extensive education, continued wise government, and an increasing fight on our part to disseminate the scientific facts and raise our levels of achievement can overcome this prejudice, which to a large extent is founded in ignorance." Unable to change the directive, Drew resigned from the blood program.

Drew continued to teach after the war. In 1950, he died in a car crash after falling asleep en route to a medical conference.

**Dr. Charles R. Drew**

# 67. THURGOOD MARSHALL (1908–1993)

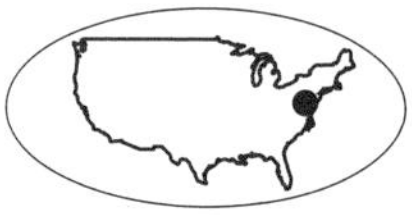

Born in Baltimore, Maryland, Thurgood Marshall became the first African American member of the U.S. Supreme Court after a career as legal counsel to the NAACP. Educated in segregated schools, where he was often forced to memorize passages of the U.S. Constitution as punishment, and Lincoln University, where he received a B.A. in predentistry, Marshall chose to study law and entered Howard University Law School.

Mentored by the brilliant designer of Howard's Law School, Charles H. Houston (see no. 55), Marshall was the obvious choice to succeed him as head of the NAACP's Legal Defense Fund in 1938. For the base of his career, Marshall fought civil rights battles using the Legal Defense Fund to slowly chip away at segregationist policies.

In 1896, the Supreme Court had established a precedent by accepting the "separate but equal" interpretation that closed Plessy v. Fergusson. Thurgood Marshall, acting on the teaching of Charles Houston, who believed that lawyers had to work as social engineers, took the case of Lloyd Lionel Games, who was

**Thurgood Marshall**

rejected by Missouri Law School, to the Supreme Court, winning the first case that put Plessy v. Fergusson into question. Arguing that no "separate" institution of "equal" value existed, Marshall convinced the Supreme Court to rule that Gaines would be admitted to Missouri University. By forcing the Supreme Court to ask the question, "What is equal?" Marshall took a step toward the case that finally ended segregation in schools.

In all, Marshall took thirty-two cases to the Supreme Court, winning twenty-nine of them. The one that outlawed any school segregation was Brown v. Board of Education. In 1954, he went into court with evidence proving that separate inherently meant unequal. Showing through psychological testing that African American students were disadvantaged by their removal from mainstream society, Marshall convinced the courts to overthrow Plessy v. Fergusson, a dangerous stumbling block for African Americans seeking equality. Though it took many court battles to prove it, there was no longer a legal leg to stand on in favor of segregation.

Winning against the Board of Education was not Marshall's only goal. He coordinated legal battles against discrimination in voting and housing. He was not only the main legal counsel for the NAACP, but he was appointed by John F. Kennedy to the U.S. Court of Appeals in 1961. None of his decisions were overturned by higher courts. He was appointed U.S. solicitor general by Lyndon B. Johnson in 1965, and Johnson appointed him to the U.S. Supreme Court in 1967, where he became a national symbol for the rights and freedoms of disadvantaged Americans.

After serving as one of the most respected members of the court, Marshall retired in 1991 and was replaced by Clarence Thomas, the second African American man to serve in the nation's highest court.

# 68. ADAM CLAYTON POWELL JR. (1908–1972)

Reverend Adam Clayton Powell Jr., chairman of the House Education and Labor Committee from 1961 to 1967, was born in New Haven, Connecticut, but raised in Harlem, where his father was the minister of Abyssinian Baptist Church. He was educated at City College of New York for two years, and then at Colgate University, from which he graduated with honors. Expecting to go on to Harvard Medical School, Powell was surprised to receive a call to the ministry. Hearing a voice ask who would succeed his father as minister of the biggest church in Harlem, Powell changed his direction and entered Teacher's College of Columbia University.

**Adam Clayton Powell Jr.**

In 1938, when he was thirty years old, Rev. Powell succeeded his father and began to use the church as a tool for social engineering. Gathering support for boycotts of businesses that wouldn't hire African Americans, Powell founded the Coordinating Committee for Employment. The committee coined the famous phrase, "Don't buy where you can't work," helping the African American community to think of itself as an economic block that could wield power with its choices in the marketplace.

In 1941, after he'd proved himself a brilliant organizer, Powell was elected to the City Council of New York. In 1944, with the support of such powerful men as A. Philip Randolph (see no. 48), Powell was named Harlem's first African American congressman. He was elected to chair the powerful House Education and Labor Committee in 1961 and helped pass the Civil Rights Act in 1964, the Economic Opportunity Act in the same year, and the Voting Rights Act in 1965. Praised by President Lyndon B. Johnson for passing the Anti-Poverty Act, the Minimum Wage Act, the Vocational Education Act, and the National Defense Education Act, chairman Powell was shocked when, in 1967, he was expelled from the House of Representatives. Founded on dubious accusations of "misuse of funds," his dismissal was a shock that went through the whole nation, ending in massive protests.

In 1967, he was reelected to his seat by his loyal supporters in Harlem, and he took his case to the courts. In 1969, Congress reversed its decision. Powell was returned to his seat. The courts upheld that Congress had acted outside its jurisdiction.

Powell was defeated in 1970 and died in 1972, described by Gil Noble as ". . . a fighter. If he did play, he worked harder than he played. Most of all, he was a fighter."

# 69. RICHARD WRIGHT (1908–1960)

**Richard Wright**

Richard Wright, born in Roxie, Mississippi, was raised in a family that suffered constantly from poverty. When Wright's father deserted the family in 1913, Richard's mother moved them to Tennessee and then Arkansas, until she became ill, and put him and his little brother into an orphanage. Rescued by his maternal grandparents, who brought the boys to Jackson, Mississippi, Richard began to attend school regularly for the first time. His mother had taught him to read, and he had decided early that he would be a writer, but the racism in Mississippi was so extreme that no opportunity would have presented itself. In desperation, Wright pulled off a small robbery and used the money from the sale of a gun and some fruit preserves to buy a ticket to Memphis.

In 1927, he moved to Chicago and started writing for *Left Front* and *New Masses*, When the Depression struck, Wright was chosen for government writing projects that kept him employed and further increased his skill. In 1935, Wright chose the Joe Louis/Max Baer fight as the subject of a short piece defining "the heart of the Negro: "Here's the fluid something that's like iron. Here's the real dynamite that Joe Louis uncovered."

In 1937, Wright moved to New York, and in 1938, his first collection of stories, *Uncle Tom's Children*, appeared. Built on his experiences with intense and violent racism in the Deep South, these stories defined the strength of the African American character trying to succeed against all odds. Well received, *Uncle Tom's Children* was followed by Wright's first, and most famous, novel, *Native Son*, which follows the character Bigger Thomas through the trials of being black in the North, held down in a "cold and distant world; a world of white secrets care fully guarded."

*Twelve Million Black Voices*, Wright's folk history, was published, quickly followed by *Black Boy* in 1945, which told Wright's own story of growing up in the rural South. Though there are questions as to its authenticity as an autobiography, the fundamental truth of *Black Boy* gained it a following as respectful as that of *Native Son*.

Wright left the United States for Paris in 1946, where he continued to write amongst a group of other intellectuals including Gertrude Stein, Jean Paul-Sartre, and Simone de Beauvoir. *The Outsider* was published in 1953, *Savage Holiday* in 1954, *The Long Dream* in 1959, and *Eight Men* in 1961.

After Wright's death in Paris, James Baldwin (see no. 85) observed: "Wright's unrelentingly bleak landscape was not merely that of the Deep South, or of Chicago, but that of the world, of the human heart."

# 70. KATHERINE DUNHAM (b. 1909)

Katherine Dunham, one of the nation's most influential choreographers, and a devoted activist for all people of African heritage, was born in Glen Ellyn, Illinois. She lost her mother when she was only three, and she and her brother were moved to South Chicago, where they stayed with an aunt while their father traveled as a salesman. Their father regained custody when Katherine was five, and the reunited family, with the addition of Annette Poindexter, Katherine's new stepmother, moved to Joliet, Illinois.

Always active, she took private piano and dance lessons from elementary school on, applying her agility and grace to athletics when she reached high school. She was elected president of the Girls' Athletic Association before attending Joliet Township Junior College, and later, University of Chicago. There Katherine began to study cultural anthropology with a passion. Pursuing her education in ethnology and African cultures, she began to mix historical tradition with her creative approach to dance. Forming Ballet Negre with dancers Ruth Page and Mark Turbyfill, Katherine launched a career as one of the finest choreographers in the United States. *Negro Rhapsody*, their debut performance at the Beaux Arts Ball in 1931, established Katherine as an expert on African dance styles, and she was chosen in 1933 to handpick 150 young dancers to perform a piece of her own design at the Chicago Century of Progress Exposition.

Dunham's work was filling a void in American dance that had never been explored before. Granted the Rosenwald Travel Fellowship in 1935, she went to Jamaica, Martinique, and Haiti to further study the origins of the Caribbean styles that formed the basis of her own original pieces.

She graduated from the University of Chicago in 1936 with a degree in anthropology and moved to Northwestern University, where she completed her doctorate under Melville Herskovitz, an anthropology expert who was also one of the first essayists of the Harlem Renaissance.

Dunham's Ballet Negre grew into the Negro Dance Group and toured more than sixty countries, bringing traditional African ritual to different nationalities in the form of Caribbean-inspired dance. Her choreographed pieces include *Ballet Fedre* (1938), *Tropics and Le Jazz Hot* (1940), *Tropical Review* (1943), *Bal Negre* (1946), *Caribbean Rhapsody* (1950), and *Bamboche* (1962). Documenting the history of African descended cultures, Dunham wrote *Journey to Accompong* (1946), *Les Danses d'Haiti* (1950), and *A Touch of Innocence* (1959).

After retiring from the stage in the 1960s, Dunham founded the Katherine Dunham Center, where she trained young people in African dance and culture. Always a supporter of African-inspired cultures, Dunham went on a hunger strike in 1992 in support of fleeing Haitians who weren't granted asylum.

**Katherine Dunham**

# 71. BAYARD RUSTIN
(1910–1987)

Bayard Rustin

Bayard Rustin, the brilliant aide to A. Philip Randolph (see no. 48) and Dr. Martin Luther King Jr. (see no. 91), added the Gandhian ideal of pacifism to the modern civil rights movement. He was born in West Chester, Pennsylvania, where he suffered at the hands of his peers. Inventing his own flamboyant character by impersonating his stepfather's Indian accent and enduring the early bullying he took from schoolmates for his extreme intelligence, Rustin sought true community in Cheyney State College and Wilberforce University in Ohio.

Attracted to socialism but disillusioned when the socialists avoided issues of racism, Rustin joined the Young Communist League in 1936. Performing in Harlem as a musician and recruiting for the Young Communist League, Rustin found a society he could charm and influence. He left the League in 1941 to join Fellowship for Reconciliation, which grew into the influential Congress of Racial Equality (CORE).

President A. Philip Randolph had been quick to spot Rustin's unique ability to organize and endure enormous pressure in order to maintain a movement. Rustin joined Randolph as his assistant and helped organize the threatened march on Washington, D.C., that convinced President Franklin D. Roosevelt to end discrimination in the military.

Always looking for the next project, Rustin was one of the first to get involved in the freedom rides. Rustin tested the new U.S. Supreme Court ruling that African Americans didn't have to sit at the back of the bus by riding in the front of an interstate bus through the South with other members of CORE. They were arrested and Rustin and his associates served twenty-two days in jail when the NAACP could not legally defend them because of lost evidence. Rustin was the first to view the punishment as a possible way to teach peace through lack of resistance.

Leaving CORE, Rustin became an aide to Dr. Martin Luther King Jr. when he and 150 others were held legally responsible for the Montgomery bus boycott. Rustin was an invaluable and brilliant activist. He helped King face arrest without resistance, drafted the original plan for the Southern Christian Leadership Conference, and assisted A. Philip Randolph in the organization of the massive 1963 March on Washington, which became the symbol for not just the civil rights movement, but all moves for liberty and equality in the United States.

Until his death, Rustin headed the A. Philip Randolph Institute in New York, where he never surrendered his belief in nonviolence and complete, uncompromised equality.

# 72. ROSA PARKS (b. 1913)

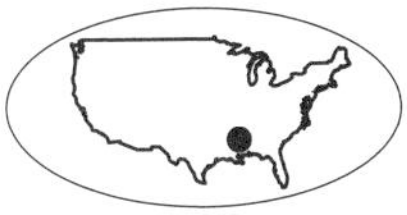

Rosa Parks is known for touching off the Montgomery bus boycott in 1955 that led to the extreme popularity of Dr. Martin Luther King Jr. (see no. 91) and the modem civil rights movement. She was born Rosa McCauley in Tuskegee, Alabama, and attended school throughout the state, living with relatives until her mother's failing health begged her return. In 1932, she married Raymond Parks and worked numerous odd jobs, joining the NAACP in the early 1940s and acting as youth advisor and secretary for the Montgomery Chapter. She later joined State President Edgar Nixon and served as his office manager.

In December of 1955, Rosa Parks, then a seamstress at a department store, refused to yield her seat on the bus to a white man as dictated by law. She was not the first woman to refuse to rise, but she was the first of impeccable reputation and upbringing. While Rosa Parks was arrested on December 1, 1955, Edward Nixon's friend Jo Ann Robinson was up all night with other members of the Women's Political Council, making the first flyers that announced a one day boycott of the Montgomery bus line on December 5, the day Rosa Parks was going to trial after being released on bail. Since 75 percent of bus riders were African Americans, the financial repercussions were damaging.

**Rosa Parks**

Robinson told Nixon of the plan while the flyers went up in African American communities. When he told the NAACP that Rosa Parks, the mild, polite, well-dressed young secretary in Montgomery, was arrested for refusing to forfeit her seat, they gathered together at Dr. Martin Luther King Jr.'s Dexter Baptist Church and decided that this would be the case they'd fight all the way to the U.S. Supreme Court. The Montgomery Improvement Association, headed by King, not only approved the boycott, but ensured that it lasted for 381 days, nearly crippling the bus line.

On December 5, Rosa Parks lost her court case but won the support of Montgomery's African American populace. As bus after bus ran through town without any black passengers, Parks's case was appealed. Finally, on December 20, 1956, the Supreme Court upheld the United States District Court ruling that segregation on public buses was unconstitutional.

Rosa Parks had begun what has been called the most important American movement since Emancipation, but she was far from retiring. In 1957, Parks moved to Detroit, Michigan, and worked with the Southern Christian Leadership Conference, which annually sponsors the Rosa Parks Freedom Award. From 1957 to 1988, she assisted U.S. representative John Conyers, and in 1980, received the Dr. Martin Luther King Jr. Nonviolent Peace Prize. In 1987, she established the Rosa and Raymond Parks Institute for Self-Development, which assists teenagers, and in 1990, was joined by three thousand government and community leaders in honor of her seventy-fifth birthday at the Kennedy Center in Washington, D.C.

# 73. JESSE OWENS (1913–1980)

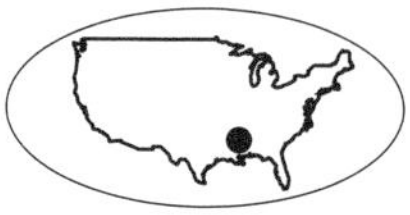

**Jesse Owens**

Jesse Owens, who took four gold medals in the 1936 Olympics, was born James C. Cleveland in Danville, Alabama, the seventh of eleven children. His family was very poor and James Cleveland, or J. C. as he was called, went to work at the age of seven picking cotton. His family moved to Cleveland, Ohio, and J. C. joined the Fairmont Junior High School track and field team. At East Technical High School, a teacher mispronounced his initials, and J. C. became Jesse for good.

Owens began running track in high school and continued while at Ohio State. In May, 1935, he competed in the Big Ten College Track and Field Championships and broke three world records. He qualified for the 1936 Olympic Games.

Owens competed at the Games in Berlin, Germany, where Adolf Hitler watched him challenge and defeat Germany's Aryan athletes. Owens took four gold medals, delivering a stinging blow to Hitler's theory of Aryan superiority. In the hundred meter, two hundred meter, long jump, and four hundred meter relay, Owens beat the world's top athletes—of all races.

Though a story circulated that Hitler snubbed Owens at the presentation ceremony, Owens denied the rumor, although he admitted that Hitler watched him with bitterness. As writer Columbus Salley pointed out, "Owens and his athletic records long outlived Adolf Hitler and the Third Reich."

When Owens returned home to the United States, he was met by a ticker tape parade. Held up as a national hero, he was particularly embraced by African American athletes, who used his example to help them break through stereotypes everywhere.

Owens, though one of the world's greatest athletes, did not have a job to support his wife and two children. Accepting a position as a playground instructor because he couldn't afford to finish college, Owens worked for thirty dollars a week until he was offered a huge prize if he could beat a racehorse in the hundred yard dash. The prize money was enough to send Owens back to college, where he completed his degree. He joined other ventures, including a chain of dry cleaners, but when his business partner disappeared, leaving Owens thousands of dollars in debt, he took a job with the Ford Motor Company.

The Owens family moved to Chicago in 1949, where Owens was able to use his reputation as a tool. Going into public relations, Owens began lecturing on athletic superiority as a tool for building teams between races. He was granted the Medal of Freedom by U.S. president Gerald Ford in 1976, four years before he died of lung cancer.

# 74. KENNETH B. CLARK
(b. 1914)

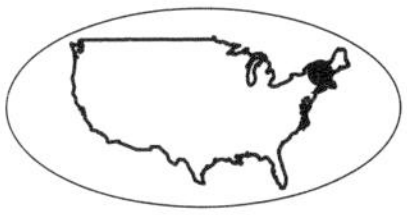

Kenneth B. Clark, who developed the psychological arguments that won the influential Brown v. Board of Education case, was born in the Panama Canal Zone where his father worked. In 1919, Kenneth and his mother returned to Harlem in New York City by themselves. Kenneth went to integrated schools and studied under inspirational mentors such as Countee Cullen, who was a teacher at Junior High School 139, and Arthur Schomburg (see no. 40), who was available as the curator of the New York Public Library's Division of Negro Literature, History & Prints.

Clark went from George Washington High School to Howard University and to Columbia, where he earned a Ph.D. in psychology. Teaching at City College of New York from 1942 on, Clark began writing about the psychological effects of segregation. Working from the theories and explanations laid down by E. Franklin Frazier (see no. 53), Clark developed proof that segregated African American children began at a disadvantage simply because they'd been excluded as a group.

In 1953, Clark published both *Desegregation: An Appraisal of the Evidence* and *Prejudice and Your Child*. In 1954, Thurgood Marshall (see no. 67) used Clark's research to sway the court in the famous Brown v. Board of Education case that found segregation unconstitutional. He used examples such as the experiment in which African American children were invited to choose from a collection of white, Japanese, and black dolls. In each instance, the children preferred the black dolls least. From these results, Marshall was able to illustrate that even from a very young age, African American children recognized that their segregation from white children was based on a judgement made against them. When the justices of the U.S. Supreme Court agreed that the evidence was sound, they could no longer accept the "separate but equal" argument of Plessy v. Fergusson.

Throughout the 1960s, Clarke added his research and analysis to the debate raging between the pacifist African American organizers following Dr. Martin Luther King Jr. (see no. 91) and the more militant followers of Malcolm X (see no. 87).

Following E. Franklin Frazier in asserting that "The natural reactions to injustice, oppression, and humiliation are bitterness and resentment," Clark defended militancy as a healthy response.

Clark's ideas, when applied to a historical context, ring true in a painful way: "I read that report . . . of the 1919 riot in Chicago, and it is as if I were reading the report of the investigating committee on the Harlem riot of '35, the report of the investigating committee on the Harlem riot of '43, the report of the McCone Commission on the Watts riot."

After the Los Angeles riots of 1992, perhaps it is even more important to recognize Clark's assertion that racism must constantly be fought because "injustice, oppression and humiliation" are often followed by acts of "bitterness and resentment."

**Kenneth B. Clark**

# 75. BILLIE HOLIDAY (1915–1959)

Billie Holiday, born Eleonora Fagan in Baltimore, Maryland, was easily one of the most beguiling singers of the 1930s, 1940s, and 1950s. She started singing publicly in Jerry Preston's Log Cabin Club at the age of fifteen, but people remember her voice from long before that. Singing at the Hot-Cha Bar and Grill in Harlem, Billie was heard by Ralph Cooper, who reported her talent to Frank Schiffman, owner of the Apollo. Getting her first gig at the Apollo in 1934, backed up by Bobby Henderson on piano, "Lady Day," who had already appeared in Paul Robeson's film *The Emperor Jones* (see no. 57) and a short film with Duke Ellington (see no. 58), "tore the house down." Already living fast and hard, Billie sang with Count Basie, Artie Shaw, and everyone else known for making music in the 1930s.

By the 1940s, Billie was singing solo all over the country. She was named *Esquire's* top female vocalist in 1944 and 1945 and had recorded with Benny Goodman, Basie, Shaw, and Eddie Heywood. Her recordings of "Lover Man" and "Strange Fruit" sold more than one million copies, and her recordings of hits "Gloomy Sunday," "I Cover the Waterfront," "Am I Blue?" and a hundred others are still considered major influences in the careers of contemporary stars.

Frank Sinatra said of her performances in the famous 52nd Street clubs in New York City: "With few exceptions, every major pop singer in the U.S. during her generation has been touched in some way by her genius. It is Billie Holiday who was, and still remains, the greatest single musical influence on me."

Currently available retrospective groupings of her work include *Billie Holiday* (1959), *The Golden Years*, two volumes of collected material from 1933 to 1942 (1962), *Lady Day*, collected work from 1935 to 1937 that appeared in the mid-1950s, and *Lady in Satin* (1958).

Though Billie's success as a singer was magical, her life was a constant struggle. Battling with drug addiction and a passion for hard living, Billie relied heavily on her friends and fellow musicians to support her. Her autobiography, *The Lady Sings the Blues*, (1956), was written with journalist William Dufty, and the movie of the same name, starring Diana Ross, was released in 1972.

**Billie Holiday**

# 76. GWENDOLYN BROOKS (b. 1917)

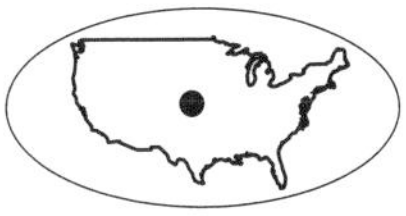

Gwendolyn Brooks, the 1949 Pulitzer Prize winning poet, was born in Topeka, Kansas, but moved to the south side of Chicago when she was one month old. Her talent with words was marked at a very early age. By the age of seven, she could fill a page with verse. By the age of thirteen, these verses were good enough for publication. "Eventide" was published in *American Childhood* magazine in 1930, and when she entered high school a year later, teachers like Langston Hughes (see no. 64) and James Weldon Johnson (see no. 36) were available to inspire and encourage her work. She graduated from Englewood High School in 1934—the same year in which *The Chicago Defender* began to publish her poems weekly—and Wilson Junior College in 1936.

Brooks's work won immediate recognition. The Midwestern Writer's Conference awarded prizes to her each year from 1943 to 1946. Her first volume of poetry, *A Street in Bronzeville* (1945), made her one of *Mademoiselle* magazine's "10 women of the year," and a Guggenheim Fellowship, awarded in 1946, made it possible for her to concentrate on writing her second volume of poetry, *Annie Allen*, which won her the 1949 Pulitzer Prize for poetry.

It has been said of Brooks's work that her first volumes are exquisitely constructed poems full of craft, but only lightly engaged with the emotional lives of individuals. Later works, including *The Bean Eaters* (1960), *Selected Poems* (1963) and *In the Mecca* (1968), are said by Norris B. Clark to show a dawning awareness of the social concerns of African Americans. The next phase of her career, yielding *Riot* (1969), *Family Pictures* (1970), *Aloneness* (1971), and *Beckonings* (1975), he says are "less devoted to craft and more concerned about pronounced statements on a black mystique, the necessity of riot (violence), and black unity."

Continuing to evolve, Brooks added *Primer for Blacks* in 1980, *Mayor Harold Washington* and *Chicago, The I Will City* in 1983, *The Near-Johannesburg Boys and Other Poems* in 1986, *Blacks* in 1987, and *Winnie* in 1988.

**Gwendolyn Brooks**

# 77. OSSIE DAVIS & RUBY DEE
(b. 1917 and 1924)

Ossie Davis and Ruby Dee, who built what W. Calvin Anderson called a "sober allegiance to a proud African oral tradition and a rich African American folklore," met for the first time through the Rose McClendon Players, a New York theater troupe. In 1947, after performing together in *Jeb Turner*, they were married. Still performing together—*Do the Right Thing* (1989), and *Jungle Fever* (1991)—Davis and Dee remain important role models for anyone interested in the artistic representation of African American culture.

**Ossie Davis and Ruby Dee**

Ossie Davis was born in Cogdell, Georgia, and educated in segregated schools, later attending Howard University, where he studied under Alain Locke. He quit Howard to pursue a career as an actor and writer in New York City but was drafted a year later, in 1942, and forced to leave the Rose McClendon Players for a term as a surgical technician in Liberia.

Ruby Dee joined the Rose McClendon Players while Davis was in the service. She had come from Harlem with a B.A. from Hunter College in 1945.

After apprenticing with the American Negro Theatre, she began to work with the Rose McClendon Players, where she met Davis on his return from Africa.

Together, they became one of the nation's key entertainment teams. They collaborated on the film *No Way Out* in 1950, the play *Alice in Wonder* in 1952, the play *Purlie Victorious* in 1961, the film version, called *Gone Are the Days* in 1963, the nine-part television series *The History of Negro People* in 1965, a record called *The Poetry of Langston Hughes* in 1964, and their own television series called *The Ruby Dee/Ossie Davis Story Hour* in 1974.

Though interested in bringing the broad scope of African American experience to all Americans through the act of storytelling in modem media, Dee and Davis were also committed activists. Associated with the NAACP, the Student Nonviolent Coordinating Committee, Dr. Martin Luther King Jr.'s Southern Christian Leadership Conference, and the Congress of Racial Equality, Davis and Dee have been tireless promoters of African American pride. Ossie Davis was the Master of Ceremonies for the 1963 March on Washington, and Dee established the Ruby Dee Scholarship in Dramatic Arts.

# 78. FANNIE LOU HAMER (1917–1977)

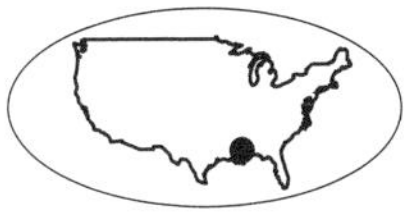

Fannie Lou Hamer, a woman who nearly lost her life while trying to register African American voters in the Deep South, was born a sharecropper in a family of twenty in Ruleville, Mississippi. In sharecropping, the land was leased from a white landowner. The family would live and work the land and split the crop with the landlord. Often all expenses, including fertilizer and seed, came from the sharecropper's share. Because the work was so hard, constant, and exhausting, children like Fannie had to leave school at a very early age to help support the family. She was picking cotton at the age of six and working full-time cutting cornstalks by early adolescence.

In 1944, Fannie left her family's farm and moved in with her husband, Peny Hamer. He too was a sharecropper, and Fannie worked with him, rising to a position of relative prominence as the plantation timekeeper.

In the early 1960s, when the South was still resistant to the growing civil rights movement, the Southern Christian Leadership Conference (SCLC) and the Student Nonviolent Coordinating Committee (SNCC) traveled through the South, encouraging African Americans to take the dangerous steps toward claiming their right to vote. Fannie Lou Hamer decided to register. She was fired from her job the day after she did. After eighteen years on the plantation with her husband, Hamer was told by her landlord that pressure from the Ku Klux Klan would be so excessive that she had to leave. Hamer fled that night. The house where she and other registered voters stayed was sprayed with bullets soon after.

With a new commitment, Hamer joined other brave people in organizing a voter registration drive that not only covered Mississippi, but grew into the Mississippi Freedom Democratic Party (MFDP). Enduring a vicious beating during a four-day detainment in Greenwood, Mississippi, Hamer learned firsthand how powerful and frightening her actions must be. After detaining her and fellow activists, police officers ordered other black prisoners to beat her with a blackjack until they were too tired to continue. Neither Hamer nor her fellow protesters gave up. If they had, men like Dr. Martin Luther King Jr. (see no. 91) might not have been able to gain the support of African Americans in the Deep South.

**Fannie Lou Hamer**

Adding to a movement that touched not just Mississippi's politics but the politics of the nation's new generation, Hamer forced Mississippi's all-white delegation at the Democratic Convention in 1964 to respond to the accusation that it adhered to traditions that deliberately and consistently excluded African Americans. This kind of pressure, steady and determined, was invaluable to the guarantee of voting rights for all Americans.

# 79. JOHN H. JOHNSON
(b. 1918)

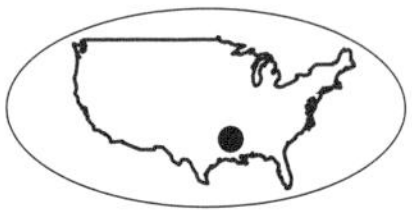

John H. Johnson

John H. Johnson, publisher of *Ebony* and *Jet* magazines, was born in Arkansas City, Arkansas. John lost his father when he was six and grew up an only son with his mother and his stepfather. In Chicago, where his family moved in 1933, John graduated from Jean Baptiste Pointe De Sable High School and attended the University of Chicago while working part time at Supreme Life Insurance Company. He then attended Northwestern University School of Commerce. Supreme Life made him editor of its in-house journal, *The Guardian*, which inspired him to formulate and publish his first piece, the *Negro Digest* (1942).

A traditional African American paper "dedicated to the development of interracial understanding and the promotion of national unity," the *Negro Digest* taught Johnson that there was a black consumer community that had not been addressed by white-owned companies. Changing his style, Johnson began to publish the stylish *Ebony* in 1945, coaxing businesses to turn to the African American community as a consumer market. Though white-owned businesses may have been the first to profit, soon African American readers were inspired to open their own businesses to fulfill the needs of African Americans, who were quickly becoming more vocal in the marketplace.

Johnson continued to build on his investment. In 1950, he published the first issue of *Tan*, and in 1951, *Jet*. Finding glamour an irresistible allure, Johnson developed his own cosmetic line, Fashion Fair Cosmetics, which was tied to the annual and international *Ebony* Fashion Show. By the late 1980s, Johnson had become a millionaire many times over, and his conglomerate business was employing nearly two thousand people in the fashion, radio, print, and cosmetics industries.

Not only did Johnson's enterprises add an African American voice to America's economic debates, but they added a sense of self to Americans who had previously been ignored. Coerced, seduced, and lured toward an elegant lifestyle by images of successful African Americans, readers began to shift their self-perception, seeing themselves reflected in the American dream in a new way—black and beautiful.

# 80. JACKIE ROBINSON
(1919–1972)

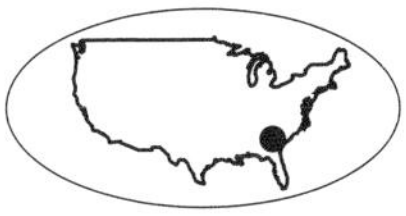

Jack Roosevelt Robinson, the first African American baseball player to see his team to the World Series, was born in Cairo, Georgia. His family lived there for a year before his father deserted them, and Jackie's mother moved them to Pasadena, California. Jackie attended Pasadena Junior College before transferring to the University of California at Los Angeles, where he was the first student to gain letters in baseball, basketball, football and track. In his third year, Robinson quit school and played for the Los Angeles Bulldogs before being drafted into the army in 1942.

Robinson applied for the Officers' Candidate School (OCS) and was turned down because of his race. Aggravated and insistent, Robinson complained to the highest level. Heavyweight champion Joe Louis, who was also stationed at Fort Riley, Kansas, used his connections to have Robinson admitted. He became a second lieutenant, later admitting how difficult it was: "I was naive about the elaborate lengths to which racists in the armed forces would go to put a vocal black man in his place."

In 1944, Robinson finally returned to his career as a baseball player in the United States. Joining the Kansas City Monarchs, an all black team playing in an all black league, Robinson came to the attention of the Brooklyn Dodgers' president and general manager Branch Rickey, who had sent scouts out into the Negro League after deciding to be the first team to desegregate baseball.

Robinson met Rickey in 1945 and promised that he could take any pressure that came from his being the first African American ball player in the white league. Already aware how extensive racism can be, Robinson was prepared when his presence nearly led to a strike.

Robinson's team members signed a petition for his removal, the president of the Philadelphia Phillies refused to play against the Dodgers while Robinson was on the roster, and the St. Louis Cardinals sent out word that they would strike.

**Jackie Robinson**

In response, the president of the National League was forced to make a statement. Coming down on the side of integration, he said to the Phillies, "If you do this, you will be suspended from the league . . . don't care if it wrecks the National League for five years. This is the United States of America, and one citizen has as much right to play as another."

Though the first years were tough and Robinson had to be twice as good as his best competitors to be accepted, in 1947 he became the first African American ball player in the World Series and was named Rookie of the Year. In 1949, he won the Most Valuable Player Award.

He retired in 1958, after a year with the San Francisco Giants, and died knowing that the world of sports was now open to players of all races.

# 81. DANIEL "CHAPPIE" JAMES JR. (1920–1978)

Daniel James Jr. was the seventeenth child of a family in Pensacola, Florida. His mother managed a school for African American children and taught her own children and others the value of leadership and a strong will. In 1937, James, nicknamed "Chappie," entered Booker T. Washington's Tuskegee Institute (see no. 24) in Alabama. Though he was a promising young man, he was expelled from the university two months before graduation because he was caught fighting with another student.

Deciding to join the army after having learned to fly an airplane at Tuskegee, James applied to a U.S. Army Air Corps advanced flying program, also at Tuskegee. In 1943, as a second lieutenant, he was assigned to the 477th Bombardment Group at Selfridge Field near Detroit. Racism was still prevalent in the armed forces, and African American officers were rarely promoted or allowed into officers' clubs and facilities, despite a regulation making segregation in these clubs illegal.

The 477th was transferred to Indiana after incidents of racial tension grew too heated. When the officers realized that racism was as rampant in Indiana, they staged a peaceful sit-in at a segregated officers' club. The protesters were arrested and charged with mutiny. When James and more than one hundred other officers came out in support of them, they too were arrested. Among the bold officers who risked their careers were Coleman Young, later elected mayor of Detroit, and the future secretary of transportation under President Gerald Ford, William T. Coleman.

In 1948, years after the officers were released by General George C. Marshall, President Harry S. Truman issued Order 9981, making segregation in the armed forces illegal.

James had begun a distinguished career. He was in the Philippines, where he was injured while saving the life of a fellow pilot. He flew more than one hundred missions in Korea and was awarded the Distinguished Flying Cross. He was made Deputy Commander for Operations for the U.S. Air Force's 81st Fighter Wing at Bentwaters, England, and later as a vice wing commander in Vietnam.

Confident and highly skilled as a leader, James faced Colonel Muammar Qadhafi, leader of Libya, in a confrontation in which Qadhafi rolled armored vehicles through Wheelus Air Force Base in 1969, demanding the United States abandon the lease that granted them the base until 1970. Qadhafi himself met James with a gun outside the gate. With obvious command, James convinced Qadhafi to withdraw, leaving the base in James's command until it was closed.

After leaving Libya, James was promoted to brigadier general at the Pentagon in 1970. Five years later, after he'd been named commander in chief of NORAD (North American Air Defense Command), he became the first African American four-star general.

**Daniel "Chappie" James Jr.**

# 82. ALEX HALEY
(1921–1992)

Alex Haley, perhaps the most successful man to employ television as a tool in teaching Americans about African American history, turned his book *Roots* into a televised miniseries that attracted a rapt national audience.

**Alex Haley**

Alex Haley was born in Ithica, New York, the first of three brothers. He grew up with not only a respectful love of storytelling, but a respectful sense of history through listening to his grandmother's stories while sitting on the porch in the evenings in Henning, Tennessee. There, she would remind the boys that their African and American history was longer than they or their parents could remember and richer in experience than they themselves could imagine.

Alex graduated from high school at age fifteen and joined the Coast Guard in 1939. He practiced writing constantly, following the formulas of other successful writers and writing on any subject. When he returned from the Coast Guard, he took up writing full-time, just as the 1960s civil rights movement was building like a storm.

From 1954 to 1956, he was a freelance writer for *Atlantic Monthly* and *Playboy*. One of his interviews for *Playboy* was with the controversial Malcolm X (see no. 87). Together, Haley and Malcolm X produced *The Autobiography of Malcolm X* in 1965, which gained massive popularity. Working on the history of one man was what inspired Haley to begin his landmark work, *Roots*.

*Roots* , which took twelve years to research, is the story of Haley's ancestral history, from before his ancestor Kunta Kinte was captured in Africa and brought on a slave ship to America all the way through the generations to Haley himself. Published in 1977, *Roots* won a Pulitzer Prize and was made into a television miniseries that immortalized not just his own family's experience, but that of millions of African Americans. By familiarizing 130 million viewers with the fascinating heritage of only one of the countless families who'd been brought to the United States, Haley led Americans of all races to begin exploring their own family histories.

Having produced what, at the time, was the most watched program ever, Haley retired to complete only one other book before his death, the novella *A Different Kind of Christmas*. His biography of Madame C. J. Walker (see no. 31) was never finished.

# 83. WHITNEY M. YOUNG, JR
(1920–1978)

**Whitney M. Young Jr.**

Whitney M. Young Jr., who transformed the National Urban League (NUL) from an employment service into a major civil rights organization, was born in Lincoln Ridge, Kentucky. He studied at the all-black Lincoln Model School and its higher institution, the Lincoln Institute, which was headed by his father. He went to Kentucky State College and graduated with an M.A. in 1947, the same year he joined the St. Paul, Minnesota, branch of the National Urban League. By 1950, Young was the executive director of the National Urban League branch in Omaha, Nebraska.

The National Urban League was formed by the 1911 merger of three separate organizations—the Committee for Improving the Industrial Conditions of Negroes in New York, the National League for the Protection of Colored Women, and the Committee on Urban Conditions. Formed to help integrate newly arrived African Americans into the society of bigger cities, the National Urban League organized programs to introduce immigrants to employers. Focused on urban social concerns, the organization worked at finding jobs for people, training them, and mediating with white businesses willing to hire black employees.

In 1961, when Young was appointed executive director of the National Urban League, Dr. Martin Luther King Jr. (see no. 91) was already active. The civil rights movement was just waiting for a catalyst—a woman like Rosa Parks (see no. 72), who was riding on a bus in Alabama and refused to give her seat to a white passenger.

When Rosa Parks's act of resistance set off the Montgomery bus boycott in 1955, the National Urban League was forced to decide whether it would remain an autonomous organization or become one that merged with the mass of Americans rising for civil liberty. It was Young's leadership that turned the National Urban League into one of the major supporters of the March on Washington in 1963.

With Young in charge, the National Urban League went through a transition that enlarged its scope of influence considerably. Persuading the organization's leadership to employ mass protest as a tool for social engineering, Young added its members to the pool of national supporters:

"The Urban League will be valueless to responsible institutions in our society if it does not maintain communication with and the respect of other responsible Negro organizations and the respect of the masses of Negro citizens."

Young remained executive director until his death in 1971, which occurred while he was attending the African American Dialogue in Nigeria. He is remembered as a man who could build bridges, and as Nancy J. Weiss said, "Young enlarged the economic opportunities available to black Americans. . . . He gave powerful whites in the private sector a means of comprehending the problems of the ghetto and, in the most successful instances, made some contribution toward their amelioration."

# 84. LEON SULLIVAN (b. 1922–2001)

Leon Sullivan, founder of the Opportunities Industrialization Centers of America (OIC), was born in Charleston, West Virginia. He became a Baptist minister while still in high school and accepted an athletic scholarship to West Virginia State College. He then studied theology at Union Theological Seminary and Columbia University based on the recommendations of his mentor, Reverend Adam Clayton Powell Jr. (see no. 68).

Sullivan learned the art of successful mass protest by watching Powell launch the "Don't buy where you can't work" campaign, encouraging African Americans to spend their income in businesses that employed African Americans. He also learned how to affect a crowd. Preaching at First Baptist Church of South Orange, New Jersey, and later at Zion Baptist Church in North Philadelphia, Sullivan spoke about God and about money. With the goal of black economic independence, Sullivan organized boycotts that convinced Philadelphia businesses to hire more than three thousand more African Americans by the year 1962.

Although the boycotts had a high rate of success, Sullivan realized he had only begun. Continuing to support only businesses that would hire African Americans, Sullivan began to train the new employees, who were being placed in jobs for which they had not been sufficiently educated. His projects came to the attention of Dr. Martin Luther King Jr. (see no. 91), who developed a new department for the Southern Christian Leadership Conference, Operation Breadbasket, that, under the leadership of Reverend Jesse Jackson (see no. 99), supported the hiring and training of African Americans in all the nation's major cities.

Meanwhile, Sullivan was gathering funds from his congregation to form a new organization, the Opportunities Industrialization Centers of America (OIC), which employed African Americans as trainers for others entering the workforce. The more Sullivan worked, the more he saw was needed. After finding jobs for African Americans, training these new employees, affecting the strongest civil rights organizations in the nation, and employing a staff of his own, Sullivan saw it was necessary to take African Americans further into the business of doing business: "We're going to have to develop literally thousands of entrepreneurs who know business for business' sake." Sullivan then began a venture capital company. His congregation invested in shopping plazas, garment factories, aerospace enterprises and apartment complexes—all owned by African Americans.

Sullivan's own business sense led him to the board of directors at General Motors in 1971 and allowed him to develop "the Sullivan Principles," which shaped U.S. policy against apartheid in South Africa. With the help of these principles, South African prisoners were freed, and American businesses that indirectly fed apartheid by feeding the South African economy pulled their support. The boycott, though it hurt South Africa's black consumers, led ultimately to the collapse of apartheid, making a multiracial democracy possible.

**Leon Sullivan**

# 85. JAMES BALDWIN
(1924–1987)

James Baldwin, one of the United States' finest writers, was born in Harlem during the electrifying Harlem Renaissance. Beginning to preach at age fourteen, following his father Reverend David Baldwin's example, Baldwin was using his youth to pull an audience when he took over as editor of his high school newspaper. After spending much of his youth in libraries writing plays, short stories, and poetry, he finally connected with other young people interested in reading and writing. He soon fell away from the church and devoted himself to writing.

Baldwin left home early and soon met novelist Richard Wright (see no. 69), who helped him secure a Eugene Saxon Memorial Trust Award. Baldwin had already begun his first novel, which was published in 1953 as *Go Tell It On the Mountain*, but he put it aside to complete a short story, "Previous Condition," which was published in 1948.

Though his talent was evident at a young age, Baldwin lived with a sense of conflict that drove him from the United States to Paris, where he found it easier to write honestly about the difficulties of being black in white intellectual circles. His first published essay, "Everybody's Protest Novel" was written in his first year in Paris, but it sharply criticized Richard Wright's *Native Son* and severed their friendship. Baldwin had a nervous breakdown due to the stress of losing his mentor, which was intensified by his financial difficulties. He recuperated in Switzerland, where he finally completed *Go Tell It on the Mountain*.

Baldwin soon returned to Europe to begin *Another Country* and the brilliant play *The Amen Corner*. He put them aside and wrote what would become his own favorite novel, *Giovani's Room*. It was followed by the collection of essays *Nobody Knows My Name* (1960), *Another Country*, completed in 1962, his exquisite and famous work, *The Fire Next Time* (1963) and *No Name in the Street* (1972). Altogether, Baldwin wrote sixteen books, along with two plays produced on Broadway, *The Amen Corner* and *Blues for Mr. Charlie*.

Even while writing in the 1950s and 1960s, Baldwin was actively involved in the social upheaval of the civil rights movement. He worked closely with civil rights groups where his influential name could be helpful. Devoted to nonviolence and the maintenance of personal integrity even in the face of ugliness, Baldwin urged African Americans to stand above their oppressors and maintain a sense of pride stronger than the insult of racism.

Baldwin continued to write until his death. His funeral, held in the Cathedral of St. John the Divine, was attended by more than four thousand mourners. Both Maya Angelou (see no. 89) and Toni Morrison (see no. 93) came to pay their respects, and they spoke of Baldwin's place in history as one of the United States' greatest writers.

**James Baldwin**

# 86. SHIRLEY CHISHOLM (b. 1924)

Shirley St. Hill Chisholm was the first African American woman elected to the U.S. Congress and the first African American to launch a campaign for a major party presidential nomination. She was born in Brooklyn, where she stayed until the age of three. Sent to her maternal grandmother in Barbados, Chisholm lived away from her parents until they could afford her education. In 1934, she returned to New York, graduating cum laude from Brooklyn College in 1946. She attended Columbia University for graduate work in elementary education and worked as a teacher before joining the New York City Bureau of Child Welfare and molding the Unity Democratic Club into an organized body for the support of district reforms.

Launching a political career in 1964 when she was elected the first African American assemblywoman from Brooklyn, Chisholm proved herself a powerful supporter of women and African Americans. She was reelected in 1965 and 1966 and launched her campaign for a congressional seat from the 12th district in 1968. Her election made her the first African American woman in Congress, and her reputation as a maverick who crossed party lines made her an excellent politician dedicated to the goals of equality.

In 1972, Chisholm used her excellent record to buoy her campaign for the Democratic Party's candidacy for the U.S. presidency. She was the first African American to make a serious attempt at the presidency, and her courage would inspire other African American leaders such as Reverend Jesse Jackson (see no. 99) to go further toward the nation's most influential political position.

**Shirley Chisholm**

Though Chisholm lost the nomination to George McGovern, she retained her position in Congress, reelected to her seat six times before her retirement in 1982. In the same year, she began teaching at Mount Holyoke College. In 1984, she founded the National Political Congress of Black Women, dedicated, as Chisholm has always been, to the elimination of racism and sexism in America and in American politics.

The NPCBW sent a delegation of one hundred American women to the Democratic Convention in 1988 to remind the nation's politicians that civil rights issues needed constant attention. Her respected career made her President Bill Clinton's choice for United States ambassador to Jamaica in 1993.

# 87. MALCOM X (1925–1965)

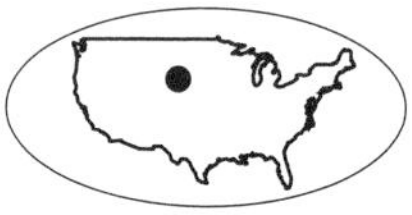

Malcolm X was eulogized by Ossie Davis (see no. 77) after his assassination as "our manhood, our living black manhood. . . . And we shall know him for what he was and is—a prince, our own black, shining prince, who did not hesitate to die because he loved us so." During the two centuries between Crispus Attucks (see no. 1) and Malcolm X, a revolution had occurred in the African American psyche. African Americans were now able to adore and admire a black leader because he embodied revolution, self-respect, and the steadfast rejection of any sublimation.

Malcolm X was born Malcolm Little in Omaha, Nebraska, the son of Reverend Earl Little, a bold Baptist preacher who moved his family to Lansing, Michigan, after receiving consistent threats from the Ku Klux Klan. In Lansing, Little's house was firebombed in response to the minister's radical notions of social justice. When Malcolm was six, his father was murdered for his egalitarian ideals. Malcolm quit school in the eighth grade and went to the streets for his education. Deeply involved in a world of drugs, crime, and prostitution in Detroit and Harlem, New York, he was jailed in 1946 for burglary. His six-year sentence taught his soul to thrive.

Malcolm joined the Nation of Islam in 1948. He studied the Honorable Elijah Muhammad's teachings and spent his time reading encyclopedias, learning new words from the dictionary, and honing his intellect on the teachings of the Black Muslims. He met Elijah Muhammad in 1952, while on parole, and was later invited to join him in Chicago. Malcolm X, using the new name given him, rose to the second highest position in the sect. For nearly twelve years, Malcolm X's pride, intelligence, and effective speeches drew new members to the Nation of Islam. Teaching African Americans to embrace rather than hate the color of their skin, find pride in their heritage and their accomplishments, and rebel against any form of racism, Malcolm X embodied the "black prince" of Davis' speech.

**Malcolm X**

In 1963, after Malcolm X's success as an orator and an organizer had earned him his own following, Elijah Muhammad decided that Malcolm X's power was out of hand. He suspended Malcolm X for ninety days after hearing him state that John F. Kennedy's assassination amounted to "chickens coming home to roost." Malcolm X responded by forming the Organization of Afro-American Unity. After a trip to Mecca in 1964, he converted to Orthodox Islam, returning to the United States with a new tolerance. He had walked among men of every color, all taking the pilgrimage required of every Muslim, and heard the words of Muhammad, "The Prophet." He changed his name to El-Hay Malik El-Shabazz and denounced Elijah Muhammad publicly.

Malcolm X ignored the death threats that followed and kept his public engagements, including the one at the Audubon Ballroom in Harlem on February 21,1965. As he began to speak to the crowd, he was shot to death. Three Black Muslims were convicted for murder, although the Nation of Islam denied any involvement. Malcolm X's death was one of the two most painful blows to the progressing civil rights movement. The second was the death of Dr. Martin Luther King Jr. (see no. 91), who opposed Malcolm X's tactics but supported his ideal of complete equality.

# 88. HARRY BELAFONTE
(b. 1927)

Harry Belafonte

Harry Belafonte, who pursued a career in movies and music while supporting the civil rights movement, was born a first generation American in New York. At age eight, he returned to his mother's native Jamaica for five years, moving back to New York to attend high school in Harlem for two years before joining the navy in 1944.

It was after his return to the United States that Belafonte fell in love with the theater. While doing janitorial work, someone gave him tickets to *Home Is the Hunter*, and Belafonte was impressed enough to join the Dramatic Workshop of the New School for Social Research in New York. He was heard singing one of his original songs during a production and was immediately signed to a jazz club called the Royal Roost. He launched his popular singing career, touring for two years before deciding to quit. He then became enamored with African inspired Caribbean folk music and its cousin calypso.

A world-class performer, Belafonte promoted these two styles and popularized African-based rhythms. Throughout the 1950s and 1960s, he crossed all lines, gaining a reputation throughout the world, developing a name that he often lent to the support of civil rights crusaders led by Dr. Martin Luther King Jr. (see no. 91). Holding a special place in the movement because he was such a celebrity, Belafonte was sought out by John F. Kennedy and became influential in forming an alliance between Kennedy and King. He organized a massive march for school integration with Bayard Rustin (see no. 71), and was instrumental in securing celebrity support for the 1963 March on Washington. His name held a lot of weight both in the African American community and the broader entertainment industry, and he was often able to enlist the popular public entertainers who swayed the opinions of so many Americans.

Even while he was assisting King and others, Belafonte was supporting a massive career as an entertainer. Appearing in *Bright Road* (1953), *Carmen Jones* (1954), *The World, the Flesh, and the Devil* (1959), *Odds Against Tomorrow* (1959), *Buck and the Preacher* (1972), and *Uptown Saturday Night* (1974), he maintained a high profile and a reputation as a dazzling screen star. But his main source of pride continued to be his involvement in the civil rights movement: "A couple off Broadway shows closed down at night to let some of the artists come, as they had done also at the March on Washington. . . . I was very proud of us, many of us black and white who did that."

Belafonte continues to be active. In 1990, he organized a reception for South Africa's new president, Nelson Mandella, and celebrated the Universal Declaration of the Human Rights of the Child with the United Nations.

# 89. MAYA ANGELOU
(b. 1928)

**Maya Angelou**

Maya Angelou, the U.S. Poet Laureate, was born Marguerite Johnson in St. Louis, Missouri. She and her brother Bailey left their parents' home for their grandmother's house when Maya was only four. She graduated from the eighth grade in Stamps, Arkansas, and she and her brother moved to San Francisco to be reunited with their mother, who had left Missouri after divorcing their father. All of these years are detailed in the first of Maya Angelou's autobiographical books, *I Know Why the Caged Bird Sings* (1970). The honest and sensitive stories of a young girl's struggle to survive made Angelou one of contemporary America's most valued writers, yet it was only the first in a lifetime of achievements.

Maya, which is what her brother called her, studied drama and dance at the California Labor School while attending George Washington High. At the age of sixteen, she had a son and faced all the moral judgements of a racist, sexist society. To describe the difficulties of being a single parent, Maya wrote *Gather Together in My Name* (1974). Intimate and vivid, it too increased her standing as a writer, as did her three other autobiographies. *Singin' and Swingin' and Gettin' Merry Like Christmas* (1976) follows her through her theatrical career, which took her all over the world on tour with *Porgy and Bess*. *The Heart of Woman* (1981) is about her maturity as an artist, and *All God's Children Need Traveling Shoes* explains her time in Africa, where she edited an Egyptian publication and lectured in Ghana. It follows her back to the United States and details her involvement in the activist 1960s.

Her first screenplay, *Georgia, Georgia* (1972), became the first produced screenplay written and directed by an African American woman.

Maya Angelou went on to make history as one of the United States' finest poets. Her published collections, including *Give Me a Cool Drink of Water 'Fore I Die* (1971), *Oh Pray My Wings Are Gonna Fit Me Well* (1975), *Still I Rise* (1978), *Shaker, Why Don't You Sing* (1983), *Poems: Maya Angelou* (1986), *Now Sheba Sings the Song* (1987), and *I Shall Not Be Moved* (1990) all preceded her brilliant reading at the inauguration of President Bill Clinton in 1992.

Named poet laureate for the nation, Maya Angelou has become more than an artist with endurance, vitality, and power. She has become a national symbol for excellence.

# 90. LERONE BENNETT JR.
(b. 1928)

Lerone Bennett Jr.

Lerone Bennett Jr. is the author of *Before the Mayflower: A History of the Negro in America*, and other texts that highlight African American history while weaving it into the story of American history. He was born in Clarksdale, Mississippi, and attended segregated schools in nearby Jackson, where he worked on his school newspaper, developing an early passion for succinct, readable prose. He edited the *Mississippi Enterprise* after graduation and went to Morehouse College, earning a B.A. in 1949. He started reporting for the Atlanta Daily World in the same year, graduating to city editor in 1952. He kept the position for a year before becoming associate editor for John Johnson's *Jet* magazine (see no. 79).

Finding himself in the Johnson Publishing Company, one of the most influential black-owned businesses of the 1950s, Bennett saw the opportunity to direct the opinions of a huge readership. When he took over the position of senior editor for the nine-year-old *Ebony* magazine in 1958, he was able to write and publish his own articles on the subject that interested him most —the history of black America.

By 1962, Bennett had developed not only a broad body of work that could stand as a major collection but a style that was both readable and exciting. He used both to create the influential text *Before the Mayflower*. Reprinted many times, this text stands as one of the finest cohesive histories in the United States. It was the first of many pieces that would earn Bennett a reputation among scholars and laypeople alike. In 1964, *The Negro Mood and Other Essays* was published. *What Manner of Man?* (1964), which tells the story of Dr. Martin Luther King Jr. (see no. 91), *Confrontation, Black and White* (1965), *Black Power, USA, The Human Side of Reconstruction 1867-1877* (1967), *Pioneers in Protest* (1968), *The Challenge of Blackness* (1972), *The Shaping of Black America* (1974), and *Wade in the Water: Great Moments in Black History* (1979) are all evidence of the illuminating quality of his work.

Continuing to communicate the complex and compelling story of African American evolution, Bennett added an up-to-date perspective to *Before the Mayflower* and released a new edition in 1982, making it a contemporary favorite of researchers and students.

# 91. MARTIN LUTHER KING JR.
(1929–1968)

Reverend Dr. Martin Luther King Jr., the most influential man ever to fight for the rights of African Americans, was born into a lineage of preachers who brought the family from slavery to a prominent social position in Atlanta, Georgia. Knowing that the church was a tool for justice and leadership, King began his career as a reverend immediately after college and ended it as a hero.

**Martin Luther King Jr.**

King led the Montgomery bus boycott, launched after Rosa Parks (see no. 72) refused to yield her bus seat to a white man in 1955. By preaching the "gospel of freedom" and organizing nonviolent protest in the tradition of Mahatma Gandhi, King maintained the boycott for 381 days, and the U.S. Supreme Court declared bus segregation unconstitutional. It was the victory the civil rights movement had been waiting for, and King was its chosen leader.

For seven years, King led boycotts, sit-ins, and marches designed to demolish segregationist policies. In 1957, King formed the Southern Christian Leadership Conference (SCLC), which became one of the dominant organizations of the movement. In 1963, King ignored an order barring protests and marched through Birmingham with a small number of supporters. He was jailed by Police Commissioner "Bull" Connor, and during his confinement he wrote the eloquent "Letter From Birmingham City Jail": "You speak of our activity in Birmingham as extreme. . . . I wish you had commended the Negro sit-inners and demonstrators of Birmingham for their sublime courage, their willingness to suffer, and their amazing discipline. . . . One day the South will recognize its real heroes."

With the support of A. Philip Randolph (see no. 48), Bayard Rustin (see no. 71), Roy Wilkins (see no. 62), President John F. Kennedy, and the nation's most popular black celebrities, King's zenith came during a speech given to more than 250,000 people who gathered in Washington to support civil rights.

King stood and defined the hope that had supported generations: "I have a dream that one day this nation will rise up and live out the true meaning of its creed: 'We hold these truths to be self-evident; that all men are created equal.' . . . When we let freedom ring, when we let it ring from every village and hamlet, from every state and every city, we will be able to speed up the day when all of God's children . . . will be able to join hands and sing, in the words of the old Negro spiritual: 'Free at last! Free at last! Thank God Almighty, we are free at last.'"

King would live to see his efforts rewarded by the Civil Rights Act of 1964, which removed the poll taxes imposed by some Southern states, promised fair hiring practices, and assured equal access to public amenities. He would celebrate the 1965 Voting Rights Act, which destroyed all arbitrary barriers to voting, and he would accept the Nobel Peace Prize in 1967, but he would tragically miss the end of his final campaign—the sanitation workers' strike of 1968. As he stepped onto the balcony of the Lorraine Motel on April 4, an assassin's bullet ended his life and ripped the heart from a movement at its zenith.

Dr. Martin Luther King Jr.'s words, far from forgotten, have inspired worldwide support of human rights. His speeches and books are always available, and his biography, *Parting the Waters* by Taylor Branch, won the Pulitzer Prize in 1988.

# 92. LORRAINE HANSBERRY
(1930–1965)

Lorraine Hansberry, playwright and civil rights activist, was born in Chicago, where her parents were always politically active. Unsatisfied with segregationist housing policies, they moved their family into an all-white neighborhood on the South Side when Lorraine was eight years old. Enduring threat, harassment, and insult, the family stayed until a lower court ruling forced them out. Unbeaten, Carl Hansberry took the case to the U.S. Supreme Court. In 1940, the segregationist policy was struck down. This was the defining event of Lorraine's youth, and it made for the subject of the first play on Broadway written by an African American woman.

Once Lorraine had graduated from Englewood High School in 1948, she attended the University of Wisconsin, leaving after two years of theater to study painting at numerous schools, including the Art Institute of Chicago. She met Paul Robeson (see no. 57), who was publishing *Freedom*, and became the magazine's associate editor in 1952.

In 1957, after her marriage to Robert Nemiroff, Hansberry wrote the first draft of what would become one of the most informative and important plays to hit Broadway, *A Raisin in the Sun*. Named after a line from Langston Hughess's poem "Harlem" (see no. 64), *A Raisin in the Sun* told the story of the young black family she had grown up in as they tried to build a home for themselves in a white neighborhood.

Not only was the play written with an extremely sensitive hand, it struck a nerve among the white and black communities poised for the explosive struggle just ahead. Succeeding in New Haven and then Philadelphia, Hansberry's first play opened on Broadway on March 11, 1959, creating an overnight sensation. It ran for more than a year and a half, won the New York Drama Critics Circle Award for Best Play of the Year, and featured artists who would change the face of the Broadway industry, including Sidney Poitier, Ruby Dee (see no. 77), and Lou Gossett.

Hansberry, an immediate celebrity, was asked to speak on civil rights and women's issues and privately with John F. Kennedy. She went on to write the text for an influential photo documentary of the era called *The Movement: Documentary of a Struggle for Racial Equality in the U.S.* (1964). Her other works include *The Sign in Sidney Brustein's Window* (1965), and after her untimely death in 1965 due to cancer, *To Be Young, Gifted, and Black: Lorraine Hansberry in Her Own Words*, adapted by her husband, and *Les Blancs: The Collected Last Plays of Lorraine Hansberry*, edited by Nemiroff and released in 1972.

**Lorraine Hansberry**

# 93. TONI MORRISON (b. 1931)

**Toni Morrison**

Toni Morrison, born Chloe Anthony Wofford in Lorain, Ohio, grew up to be one of the most significant novelists of this age. Born during the Depression, she experienced the extreme poverty that African Americans often faced. She was the daughter of sharecroppers who moved to Ohio after losing their land in Greenville, Alabama.

Morrison was an excellent student who completed her B.A. at Howard University in 1953 and her M.A. at Cornell University two years later. She began teaching at Texas Southern University in 1955 but left her post to teach at Howard University from 1957 to 1964. She wrote short stories, changed her name to Toni Morrison, and in 1964 began to edit textbooks for Random House. She was promoted to senior editor of the trade division, moved to New York City, and wrote her first novel, *The Bluest Eye*, in 1969. Based on the story of a black girl who yearns for a white concept of beauty, *The Bluest Eye* touched a new chord in American readers.

It was followed by *Sula* (1973) and *Song of Solomon*, which won the National Book Critics Circle Award in 1977. The following year, President Jimmy Carter appointed Morrison to the National Council of the Arts. *Tar Baby* (1981) was followed by *Beloved*, which won the 1987 Pulitzer Prize for Literature. *Jazz* won the 1993 Nobel Prize for Literature.

While writing and editing for Random House, Morrison still continued to teach. From State University of New York in 1969 to Yale University in 1975 to Bard College from 1979 to 1980, Morrison used her poetic, intimate voice to explore "things that had never been articulated, printed or imagined . . . about black girls, black women."

In 1984, Morrison retired from textbook publishing and became the humanities chair at the State University of New York at Albany. She left when Princeton University offered her the Robert Goheen Professorship on the Council of the Humanities, making her the first African American woman writer to hold a named chair at an Ivy League university.

Along with her novels, which are held up among the nation's best, Morrison wrote a play, *Dreaming Emmet*, and published a book of essays, entitled *Playing in the Dark* (1992).

# 94. BILL COSBY
(b. 1937)

Bill Cosby, whose highly accessible humor has endeared him to fans of all races, was born in Philadelphia, Pennsylvania. He attended Central High School for a year before transferring to Germantown High School, where he dropped out after his sophomore year in 1952. Cosby worked odd jobs for three years before joining the U.S. Navy. He left the military and accepted an athletic scholarship to Temple University in 1960, where he played football and worked part time as a bartender. While warming up audiences at The Underground, Cosby discovered the appeal of his own comedic voice. He went to work at Greenwich Village's Gaslight in 1962 as a stand-up comedian and quit Temple to tour the nation.

After his marriage to Camille Hanks in 1964, Cosby joined the cast of "I Spy," for which he was awarded television's highest acknowledgement, the Emmy. The show was cancelled in 1968, but Cosby was a successful star by then. He starred in the popular "Bill Cosby Show," as well as other projects that kept him in the public eye, before launching the phenomenally successful "Cosby Show" in 1984. This television sit-com proved how much had changed in the public definition of race. Based on the family of a successful doctor and the aches and pains of growing up together, "The Cosby Show" became the most popular show on television and held that position for years before signing off in 1992.

Bill Cosby's family humor highlights how little difference there is between contemporary black and white Americans. With familiar concerns, familiar pleasures, and familiar affections, Cosby has shown that African Americans are first and foremost Americans.

Cosby continues to use his humor as a way of bridging societal gaps. Publishing three best-sellers, *Fatherhood* (1985), *Time Flies* (1987), and *Love and Marriage* (1989), Cosby is constantly finding the humor in all American life, even the most innocent events of the American family.

**Bill Cosby**

Although he's achieved immense success and popularity among all Americans, Cosby has chosen to support the institutions that successfully raise the standard of living for African Americans still struggling in a volatile economy. Giving twenty million dollars to Spelman College in 1988, Bill and Camille Cosby have supported the idea that African Americans must use their success to support others who are attempting to improve their lives.

# 95. COLIN POWELL (b. 1937)

Colin Powell

Colin Powell, appointed by former president George H. Bush to chairman of the Joint Chiefs of Staff, was born in Harlem in New York City. He went to Morris High School in the South Bronx and College of New York, from which he graduated in 1958 with a B.S. in geology. He also joined the Reserve Officers Training Corps, where he became a second lieutenant upon graduation. He served in Vietnam and entered George Washington University after two tours of duty. He married Vivian Johnson in 1963

Graduating with an MBA in 1971, Powell was educated in more than just business. He had received a White House Fellowship the same year and had already been exposed to the daily politics of Washington. Though he continued to climb through the ranks in the military from 1972 to 1978, it was the Jimmy Carter administration that brought him back into the complex world of White House politics. As executive assistant to the secretary of energy and then as senior military assistant to the deputy secretary of defense successively from 1979 to 1986, Powell began a new ascent. He was sent to Frankfurt, Germany, where he was named commanding general of a U.S. Army Corps before returning to assist Frank Carlucci, the president's national security advisor, and the National Security Council.

When Carlucci was promoted to secretary of defense, Powell succeeded him as national security advisor. Through successive positions, Powell had learned how to affect national policies on security and trade. He was also a respected advisor on domestic issues such as education and the environment.

Already a visible, key player in national and international affairs, it was President George H. Bush who promoted Colin Powell to "the most powerful military position in the world," as writer Columbus Salley wrote. In 1989, Colin Powell was named chairman of the Joint Chiefs of Staff. It was the highest honor a military man could receive.

When Iraq invaded Kuwait in August, 1990, it was Powell who was in control of organizing Operation Desert Storm, ultimately forcing Iraqi troops out of that oil-rich country in February, 1991. Less than a month of full warfare waged by the Allies against Iraq was all it took to end an internationally threatening situation.

Colin Powell was reappointed by President George Bush in 1991 and retired in 1993.

Colin L. Powell became the sixty-fifth Secretary of State on January 20, 2001, under President George W. Bush.

# 96. MARIAN WRIGHT EDELMAN

(b. 1939)

Marian Wright Edelman

Marian Wright Edelman, dedicated civil rights activist and founder of the Children's Defense Fund (CDF), was born in Bennettsville, South Carolina. She was the daughter of parents who advocated grassroots social programs, and she founded the Wright Home for the Aged, which Marian's mother ran. Marian attended segregated schools and excelled at Spelman College, where she was offered a stipend to study at the Sorbonne in Paris and the University of Geneva in Switzerland. She returned to Spelman in 1959 for her senior year, during which she participated in the sit-ins and protests that were integrating the South. She graduated valedictorian in 1960 and was so engaged with the civil rights movement that she dropped her plans to study international relations and went to Yale University Law School instead.

She was active in a voter registration drive in Mississippi during 1963, interned with the Jackson, Mississippi NAACP, and headed the NAACP Legal Defense and Educational Fund between 1964 and 1968. In 1968, the Field Foundation awarded her a grant that allowed her to found the Washington Research Project, which began Wright's lifelong journey to understand the effects of poverty on children and find the solutions to the problems faced primarily by African Americans.

Wright's research was so powerful that she founded the CDF to affect political policy and secure the funds and the political support that could alleviate the pressures of poverty on America's children. She viewed CDF's mission as educating Americans about how to take preventative action in the areas of health, education, child care, youth employment, child welfare, and family support services. In 1987, the CDF introduced the Act for Better Child Care, bringing children's health to the forefront of the discussion on how to strengthen the United States in a newly globalized economy.

Edelman has received more than thirty-five awards for her work, including the Albert Schweitzer Humanitarian Prize (1988), and has produced a published body of work on the needs and concerns of the nation's quietest population. *Children Out of School in America* was published in 1974, *School Suspensions: Are They Helping Children* in 1975, *Portrait of Inequality: Black and White Children in America* in 1980, *Families in Peril: An Agenda for Social Change* in 1987, and *The Measure of Our Success* in 1992.

# 97. WILMA RUDOLPH
(1940–1994)

**Wilma Rudolph**

Wilma Rudolph, who overcame crippling polio to win three gold medals in track events at the 1960 Summer Olympics, was born in Bethlehem, Tennessee, seventeenth of nineteen children. Born prematurely, she had to fight for her life from the beginning. Wilma spent her early childhood bedridden, susceptible to everything, and surrounded by an enormous family. Though Wilma was always struggling to regain her health, the hardest fight was the one she waged against polio, which struck when she was four years old. Told she would never walk again, Wilma was confined to her bed, but her parents refused to accept defeat and waged a family war against the effects of the disease.

Every member of the family was put to the task of massaging and exercising Wilma's leg muscles, performing an early form of physical therapy. Wilma's mother took time off from her job as a maid to drive her daughter to a specialist 90 miles (145 km) away once a week, and slowly, through constant effort, Wilma began to improve. By the time she was eight, she could walk again with the help of a brace. Soon after that, she was able to walk without the brace, though she had to wear a special shoe. Finally she could go to school. Her limp was pronounced at first, but Wilma accepted challenges like a winner. She began playing basketball with her many brothers (strengthening her muscles, agility, and balance) and practicing by herself once she'd worn them out. At age eleven, Wilma performed what would have seemed like a miracle to the doctors who had doubted her. She took off her special shoe and played basketball barefoot, proving once and for all that she had mastered the use of her legs.

Basketball was the sport she had taught herself to excel in, and she kept with it, becoming an all-state high school champion when she was fifteen. She scored 803 points in the space of twenty-five games, breaking the state record for girls' basketball. At the same time, she was excelling in track and field.

As a senior in high school, Rudolph qualified for the 1956 Olympics, held in Melbourne, Australia. She won a bronze medal in the 400-meter relay and came home determined to go even further. She qualified again in 1960, and this time went to Rome, Italy, where she not only won a gold medal in the 400-meter relay, but also in the 100- and 200-meter relays. Voted U.S. Female Athlete of the Year by the Associated Press, Wilma Rudolph returned to the United States as "the fastest woman in the world."

# 98. BILL GRAY (b. 1941)

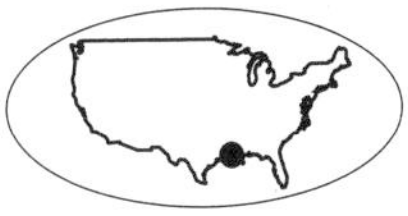

Bill Gray, who was majority whip of the Democratic Party in Congress before becoming president and CEO of the United Negro College Fund (UNCF), was born in Baton Rouge, Louisiana. He followed the example of his father, Dr. William Herbert Gray II, who was president of Florida Normal and Industrial College (1941-1944) and Florida A&M College (1944-1949) and left to become the pastor of the Bright Hope Baptist Church in Philadelphia.

Gray grew up with his father's passion for both religion and education. He graduated from Franklin & Marshall College in 1963 with a B. A. and from Drew Technology Seminary in 1966 with a Master of Divinity degree. He received a Master of Theology degree from Princeton in 1970 and succeeded his father and grandfather as pastor at the Bright Hope Baptist Church after his father's death in 1972.

Gray was a dedicated organizer, building nonprofit housing corporations and running for Congress for the first time in 1976. Though he lost to the incumbent Robert Nix, he ran again in 1978 and was elected to the Second Congressional District for six consecutive terms, retiring by choice to preside over the UNCF in 1992.

Gray's presence in Congress was always influential. In 1985, when he was elected to chair the House Budget Committee, it was because his reputation had led him to distinction as a man capable of passing a budget of trillions of dollars through Congress. Not only did he affect the national budget, but he did so with a special care for programs related to education, minimizing poverty, and assisting those in need.

Gray was also a member of the Subcommittee on Foreign Operations, where he was able to author the Anti-Apatheid Acts of 1985 and 1986, both of which demanded that apartheid be abolished in South Africa if U.S. relations were to remain friendly. In 1992, when apartheid was abolished in South Africa and the presidency was won by Nelson Mandela, Gray was one of the men who could take credit for aiding the transition.

In 1989, Gray was elected to the third most powerful position in the Democratic Congress—majority whip. Though he would have been able to affect national policy indefinitely, Gray decided to retire from Congress in 1991 to become the CEO of the United Negro College fund, causing a considerable shock in Washington.

What led Gray to his new career was his unfailing belief in education. Facing a world that he calls "a culture out of control," he took the most meaningful position possible in the struggle toward educational, economic, and civil equality. Realizing that African Americans face difficult challenges, he put the strength of his name and his reputation behind the thing he had undying faith in—education.

**Bill Gray**

# 99. JESSE JACKSON (b. 1941)

**Reverend Jesse Jackson**

Reverend Jesse Jackson, founder of the Rainbow Coalition and two-time candidate for the Democratic Party's presidential nomination, was born in Greenville, South Carolina, where he excelled in high school football, baseball and basketball. He graduated in 1959 and accepted a football scholarship to the University of Illinois. Citing racism as the reason, Jackson left Illinois for the predominantly black North Carolina A&T College.

While at A&T, Jackson earned a reputation for being more than just an athlete. As student body president, he was a fearless public demonstrator, leading sit-ins that sometimes ended in massive arrests, while proclaiming, "I'll go to jail and I'll go to the chain gang if necessary." He graduated in 1964 and attended Chicago Theological Seminary at the University of Chicago in 1965, following in the footsteps of some of the finest African American leaders.

In 1965, Jackson met Dr. Martin Luther King Jr. (see no.91), who became his mentor until King's death in 1968. King named Jackson head of Operation Breadbasket, a highly influential program within the Southern Christian Leadership Conference (SCLC) designed to increase the economic power of African Americans by involving them in white businesses that catered to black consumers. Extremely charismatic as an organizer and as a leader of boycotts, Jackson was able to expand the Chicago-based program until Operation Breadbasket was busy finding jobs for African Americans in every major city of the nation.

Jackson left Operation Breadbasket in 1971 and founded PUSH (People United to Save Humanity), which dedicated itself to increasing the economic power of African Americans. The spin-off program that Jackson launched in 1976, PUSH for Excellence, was designed on the principle that education was the greatest tool to success. Increasing the quality of African American education was directly tied to increasing their power in American society while improving the quality of life.

Jackson expanded his interest to international issues, meeting with leaders in the Middle East in hopes of effecting peace. His main successes came in 1984, when he used his friendship with Syrian leader Hafez al-Assad to free navy pilot Robert Goodman and his popularity in Cuba to free forty-eight American and Cuban prisoners.

In the same year, Jesse Jackson ran for the first time for the Democratic party's presidential nomination. Though he launched a highly visible campaign with the support of his "Rainbow Coalition," which focused on the needs of Americans of all colors and gained support, he lost to Walter Mondale. Running again in 1988, he lost to Michael Dukakis. Summing up the difference in the two campaigns, Jackson said, ". . . There were victories all over the place, and there are still victories to be had, after all. Mondale got 6.7 million votes and won; I got seven million and lost; Dukakis got nine million." Because more Democrats voted in 1988, the seven million votes, which would have beat Mondale in 1984, weren't enough to beat Dukakis in 1988.

Jackson has continued his influence upon American society with numerous public appearances.

# 100. MUHAMMAD ALI (b. 1942)

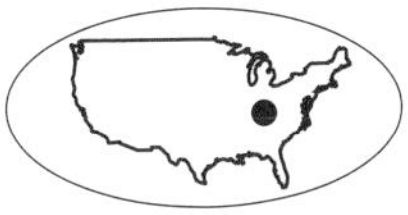

Muhammad Ali

Muhammad Ali, who was called "arguably the greatest fighter of all time" by Thomas Hauser, was born in Louisville, Kentucky, where he took up boxing at age twelve. His bicycle had been stolen, and Ali, named Cassius Marcellus Clay Jr. at birth, was learning to fight in order to beat up the kid who stole it. As Columbus Salley wrote, "By the time he finished high school, Ali had fought 108 times as an amateur boxer, won six Kentucky Golden Gloves championships, two National Golden Glove tournaments, and two national Amateur Athletic Union titles." Already considered the best in the world, Ali made it official in 1960, the year he took the Gold Medal at the Olympic Games in Rome, Italy.

Returning to the United States to turn professional, Ali stole some of Georgeous George's rhetoric and picked up the talk that made him famous. Constantly proclaiming "I'm pretty, I'm the best. . . . Float like a butterfly, sting like a bee."

Ali gained national popularity and an international reputation in 1964, when he beat the heavyweight champion Sonny Liston, becoming the new champion of the world. The day after he won the title, Ali publicly announced that he had joined the Nation of Islam and accepted the new name bestowed on him by the Honorable Elijah Muhammad. From then on, he was Muhammad Ali.

Taking a firm stand in his open acceptance of the Black Muslim faith, Ali was prepared for the resistance that might come from his fans, but it was difficult to accept the U.S. Army's response. Drafted in 1967, Ali refused to fight in the Vietnam War because of his religion. Not only was his refusal made public but so was his bold argument against the war: "My enemy is the white people, not Viet Cong or Chinese or Japanese. You're my foes when I want freedom. You're my foes when I want justice." Convicted for draft evasion, Ali was stripped of his title, and his boxing license was revoked. In 1971, the U.S. Supreme Court reversed the decision, granting him conscientious objector status. His vindication added a new fire to his quest to regain his title. Fighting and beating George Foreman in 1984, Ali remained a nationally beloved champion until Leon Spinks took the title in February of 1978. In September of the same year, Ali fought Spinks again, won the title back, and remained undefeated until his retirement in 1981.

When he left the world of boxing, he said, "Now my life is really starting. Fighting injustice, fighting racism, fighting crime, fighting illiteracy, fighting poverty, using this face the world knows so well." He suffers from Parkinson's Disease.

# TRIVIA QUIZ

1. Two African Americans have tried to capture the Democratic candidacy for the U.S. presidency. Who were they? (See nos. 86 and 99.)

2. The Harlem Renaissance was an art movement that developed after World War II in New York City. Who were some of the many authors involved? (See nos. 32, 36, 37, 47, 52, 61, and 64.)

3. The 1963 March on Washington brought more than 250,000 Americans to Washington, D.C. in support of civil rights. What were the two pieces of civil rights legislation that passed within the next two years? (See nos. 62, 68, and 91.)

4. There were two important movements that sprang up near the end of the nine teenth century. One turned into the National Association for the Advancement of Colored People. The other was based around a famous learning institution. What were the names of these two movements? How did they differ? In what ways were they the same? (See nos. 24 and 32.)

5. Why did the Underground Railroad help slaves move safely to the North? (See no. 15)

6. Many musical forms emerged based on old spirituals brought from Africa. Name a couple of the forms that became popular and the musicians who popularized them. (See nos. 34, 54, 60, 75, and 88.)

7. Matthew Henson, Dr. Charles Drew, and Dr. Daniel Hale Williams were all responsible for being the first in the world to discover something. What did each of them do? (See nos. 25, 30, and 66.)

8. What was "the Red Record?" (See no. 27.)

9. Which husband and wife team met for the first time in the theater and went on to serve the civil rights movement? In what ways did they help improve the lives of African Americans? (See no.77.)

10. What was the doctrine of Plessy v. Fergusson? How did the Brown v. Board of Education Supreme Court case over turn it? (See nos. 55, 56, 67, and 74.)

11. Madame C. J. Walker was the first female African American millionaire. How did she do it? (See no. 31.)

12. One athlete won four gold medals for his performances in the Olympic Games. Another overcame polio and won three gold medals. Who were they and in what years did they compete? (See nos. 73 and 97.)

13. Malcolm X and Dr. Martin Luther King Jr. were both great orators who believed in civil rights, but they differed in their beliefs about how to achieve them. What were the differences? (See nos. 87 and 91.)

# TRIVIA QUIZ

14. How did Alex Haley affect 130 million television viewers? Who were his two other books about? (See no. 82.)

15. Many of the people included here were journalists. Name three people who started their own publications. What were the names of their publications, and what were they about? (See nos. 8, 12, 14, 21, 32, 35, 38, 48, 61, and 79.)

16. Who was the most important African-American filmmaker of the early twentieth century? How did he differ from other filmmakers of the period? (See no. 45.)

17. How did First Lady Eleanor Roosevelt help Marian Anderson break through racial boundaries? (See no. 63.)

18. Colin Powell made world history in this decade. How did he do it? (See no. 95.)

19. What event led to the founding of the first national African American church? (See no. 6.)

20. What was the black Back-to-Africa movement? (See nos. 12, 23, and 46.)

21. In all fields, including politics, education, entertainment, religion, science, the arts, and medicine, there are men and women who have become our modem day heroes. Name one person from each field who inspires you.

# INDEX